TALES of the RAILS

by Ernie Ross

Bristol

Broadsides

Acknowledgements:

Thanks to:	Avon County Reference Library, Bristol City Museum, South West Arts, British Rail.
Produced by:	Bristol Broadsides (Co-op) Ltd. 110 Cheltenham Road, Bristol, BS6 5RW.
Copyright	©Ernie Ross and Bristol Broadsides. (1984)
Typesetting by:	Set Left (TU), Cardiff.
Printing by:	Fingerprints Community Litho (TU), Cardiff.
ISBN 0 906944 17 1	Paperback
ISBN 0 906944 18 X	Hardback

FP.954

Bristol Broadsides is a member group of the Federation of Worker Writers and Community Publishers.

The author and publishers would like to thank the following for their permission to reproduce illustrations:

British Rail: Pages 14, 21, 40 (bottom), 53, 67, 73, 87, 92.

City of Bristol Museum and Arts Gallery (Woodfin Collection): Pages 8, 11, 35, 40 (top), 44, 70, 89.

Avon County Reference Library: Pages 16, 17, 49, 50.

CONTENTS.

Introduction

I was born in 1911, the first son of a locomotive shedman, in a terraced house alongside the tracks of the GWR (Great Western Railway) and the L&SWR (London & South Western Railway) at Salisbury. Soon after the outbreak of the First World War my father enlisted, and we moved to a village near Swindon. At the end of the war, we returned to Salisbury when my father was demobilised, and he returned to his railway duties in the GWR shed there. When I was about ten years old, I went with a friend of my own age to the shed with a message for my father. He had a 28XX class engine on the turntable and he demonstrated to us the perfect balance of the turntable, by allowing the two of us to turn the great locomotive unaided and with ease (these locos exceeded 100 tons).

We next moved to Trowbridge, until the shed there was closed, when we moved to Westbury.

I started railway work as a porter at Trowbridge in 1936, and we moved to Bristol Temple Meads in 1939. At the outbreak of war I was sent to Devizes as a shunter (class 4), and left there in 1940 to go to Yeovil Pen Mill as shunter (class 3). Soon after the war finished I was appointed goods guard at Wells, where I remained for about ten years until redundancy forced my return to Bristol Temple Meads. During my time at Bristol I worked every class of train from local freight to the prestige expresses such as the Cornishman and the Blue Pullman. About 1973 failing health made me leave the trains, and I moved into telephone enquiries to complete my service up to pension age in 1976.

While I was at Trowbridge a fine old goods guard named Mark Cannon persuaded me to join the National Union of Railwaymen, of which I remained a member until the day I retired. I held a couple of minor offices, and might have had more senior posts, but I followed the advice given me by a very astute head shunter. He said, 'Always remember that all union branches need informed critics. It is one of the most useful functions you can perform for your branch, although the chairman will not often thank you for it.' During all my time in the union, the NUR had an official strike of **one day,** and on that day I was on holiday abroad.

When I started in 1936, we had one week's annual leave, and two Bank Holidays, Good Friday and Christmas Day. Of course we could be called upon to work both these days, but we would get the enhanced rate of time-and-a-half which meant that, in effect, we worked for half rate, since we would be paid for staying home. I saw annual leave increase to two and then three weeks per year. The Bank Holidays increased to seven, and if we worked any of them we were granted leave in lieu. Sunday's enhanced rate rose from time and a quarter to time and three quarters, (double time in a few selected instances).

I started work at £2 a week (of 48 hours) rising to £2.10s by the outbreak of war. On retirement in 1976 I was receiving about £40 for a week of 38 hours.

The stories in Tales of the Rails cover the period 1936-76. The dates quoted are very necessary because contrary to general belief the railways of Britain have faced and still face constant change. The organisation of the companies from heaven knows how many separate concerns to the four main-line groups had already taken place, but the time includes nationalisation. In these tales will be found some of the earlier diesel cars, the great steam locomotives, and the Blue Pullmans. It is clear therefore that dating such tales is essential because they can only be true of the period quoted. Railwaymen were adaptable because they had to be. These years saw the change in freight carrying, from a point where freight trains occupied every gap between the passengers, to their virtual disappearance today. Stations by the score have gone and sometimes whole tracks have ceased to exist.

I was mainly concerned with what is now the Western Region, but I came into contact with the Southern Region, the London Midland Region, and the Somerset and Dorset Joint (now extinct).

The railwaymen watched the disappearance of most of the semaphore signals (called boards or sticks) to the present, where five signal-boxes, now called panels, control the whole of the original track from Paddington to Bristol by means of colour light signals. That track itself has been altered out of all recognition. The period started with the 60 foot bullhead rail and ended with flatbottomed rails ten times as long and with chamfered joints. Yet it is doubtful if many passengers realise that the clackety-clack of the 60 foot joints has gone for ever.

Vacuum brakes on passenger trains are on the way out, the air-brake has largely replaced them. During the period, the slip coach disappeared. Who now even knows what they were? The rules of the railways were revised and 'simplified' into a book twice as large as the original. Still some propagandists say there is no change on the railways.

If in these tales the characters sometimes appear frivolous it should be remembered that some light relief is absolutely essential to such a serious business as running a railway. Most names and many places have been changed in order not to give offence, or enable characters to be too easily identified, but every story is based on fact, and in most cases is 100% true.

Ernie Ross

Tales from the 1930s

A Private Recital

The Manchester van used to stand in the bay platform, and the Portsmouth to Bristol passenger train would pick it up daily on the rear. It used to be about half loaded at its station of origin, and pick up traffic all the way to Manchester. One day the "Bristol" was running late and the upside staff were sitting in the van awaiting its arrival. Vernon was getting very bored. The others were humming and singing quietly; the doors were pulled together but not fully closed. Vernon said, 'That's not the way to sing that, listen to me, the only man envied by Richard Tauber.' He started on the popular song of the day singing it in the style of an operatic tenor,

Be sure it's true when you say I love you. He paused to tell us, 'I had to turn down a season at La Scala, they just were not good enough for me -

It's a sin to tell a lie - Vernon was in top gear now and he truly had a good voice -

Many a heart has been broken - with much operatic gesture -

Just because these words were spoken - Vernon was rivalling any Italian tenor now -

I love you yes I do. I love you - down on one knee now, hand upraised -

If you break my heart I'll die - Vernon's voice now had the power of a force nine gale -

So be sure it's true when you say I love you - on a note only to be reached by a high ladder -

It's a sin to tell a lie high . . . . Mac kicked the van doors open, Vernon gazed in astonishment at the forty or more passengers who had been listening to his "recital". Then as they gave him a hearty round of applause, Vernon jumped from the van and ran to the lamproom where he remained until the Bristol had gone.

Cleaning Windows

The passimeter office was an early labour-saving device. It consisted of a small portable building blocking the entrance and/or exit from a railway platform. It had a timber lower body and glass above. There was a small gate on either side which the clerk could lock or unlock from inside to permit passengers to pass, provided they had their tickets.

Masses of ticket racks covered most of the glass. It was necessary, because of this, to use artificial light most of the time. In the case I shall quote, this lighting was by gas and it caused the glass to get very dirty. There were eight porters at the station and each week one of them was supposed to clean the passimeter windows. Cleaning outside wasn't too bad - but inside it meant unhanging the ticket racks and cleaning a bit at a time. It disturbed the booking clerk and was a nuisance all round. Frequently, if he was busy, he refused to be disturbed, and the porter would just clean the outside and scram.

The station master had his knife into Jim, and when it was Jim's turn to clean windows, he used to make sure that he cleaned inside the passimeter. Of course by the time it was Jim's turn there was eight weeks' grime on the inside. There wasn't anything much he could do about it, but one thing he did do. The station master's nickname among the staff was Rasputin, and Jim made up rhymes about him, and left them all over the station. They were found by passengers as well as the staff and the nickname Rasputin was soon well known to the passengers and the boss couldn't prove a thing, though he suspected a lot.

During another week of the porters' roster, it was a duty to read the gas meters at the station, signal-boxes and the outlying halt, and record them in a special book. It was a job which Jim carried out with accuracy and some interest. He had been to the meter at the little halt, and was sitting waiting for the local train to take him back to the main station. He was thumbing through the readings when he noted that the gas consumption was rising steadily during the spring when it should have been falling. When he got back to the main station he studied the results for the other meters. They were all alike; steadily rising consumption during the spring, and now in early summer, when some should be showing a nil rise, the rise was continuing.

He knocked on Rasputin's door and was gruffly told to come in. He laid the facts before Rasputin who said, 'Well, what do you suppose is the reason for it?' Jim said, 'leaks', and so it proved. The gas linesman spent only a few hours exploring the installation, and when his thumb went through a rusted pipe he condemned almost all of it.

Some weeks later when it had all been renewed and tested, Rasputin sent for Jim, who stood to attention in front of his desk. Rasputin said, 'Well Smith, the company is of course pleased with your work in discovering the gas leaks, and I have instructed to tell you so. But don't get any false ideas of your cleverness. When your turn comes round I shall see that you clean the passimeter windows - outside and in!'

Station staff, probably 1900s, including locomotive crew, shunters, porters, guards, clerical staff, station master.

Fire Drill

Rasputin had an urge to conduct fire drills, and if Jim Smith was on duty, he would arrange to have a fire drill during what would otherwise be a mid-morning break. It became a nuisance, because in order to get Jim on fire drill, all the rest of the staff had to be stirred up with him. One day, Rasputin decided to find how far the hoses could project the water in every direction. So Jim and Vernon had to couple the hoses to the stand-pipe in the middle of the station approach. Then they coupled the two sets of hoses on end.

The water jet would not reach the goods shed but that didn't matter too much because there was another stand-pipe near the goods office. But in aiming at it, Jim and Vernon managed to thoroughly wet the checker who was collecting wagon labels at the time. And joy oh joy! Rasputin had to admit that he had ordered it and to apologise. So he ordered the pair to see if the jet would reach the bay sidings, which were right across the station. Unfortunately no-one could see where the water was going to, because the upside buildings blocked the view.

So Rasputin ordered his pair of slaves on to the almost flat parcels office roof. 'Now see how far the jet will reach,' he said. The jet reached right over to the coaches in the bay sidings, and satisfactorily washed their roofs. The chimney of the refreshment rooms' kitchen was smoking steadily. Miss Smith or Miss Davis would be preparing lunches. They did a few cooked lunches every day including their own. Jim nudged Vernon. 'Lift the jet a little,' he said. They lifted the jet and the water fell in a considerably shortened arc and down the chimney it went.

Immediately there was a scream and some very unladylike cursing; the kitchen door was flung open violently and out rushed two very black ladies, dressed in black and white striped clothes. But after a little while Rasputin discovered that they were Miss Smith and Miss Davis liberally camouflaged with soot. It was soon very clear to him that they didn't care much for the camouflage. They marched over the footbridge, out into the station yard, grabbed Rasputin by one arm each, marched him back to his own office, and shut the door. Jim and Vernon heard, with great satisfaction, two raised voices - both female. The two ladies eventually came out, closed the refreshment room for the afternoon, and took the station taxi into town, where Rasputin had made hurried telephone reservations for baths, new underwear and hair-dos. The staff quarters at this station had no bathroom and the ladies had to use the public baths. This was the last time there was a fire drill during Jim's service at that station.

The Foreman's Hat

Each summer, in the old days, the railways ran a great number of extra trains and advertised excursions. Indeed on an average Saturday the number of trains running would be at least twice that of any weekday. To work these trains the companies promoted other staff such as porters on a temporary basis. They were called summer guards and their pay was a rise of 25% over the porters' wage though still 25% below the guards' rate. But it was sufficiently attractive to the lower paid men that the companies could pick and choose from the numerous applicants. Jim Smith decided he could do well without Raputin's knife in his back for a bit and applied for a summer guard's job. The district inspector, a hard but just man, recommended him, and he was sent for in May to pass the rules examination, and to get some route knowledge. This was the summer of 1939. Jim revelled in the work, and loved the adventure of not knowing what the next day would bring. He made up his mind that if there was any way at all of avoiding it he would not go back to Rasputin.

By late August the threat of war had become obvious, and of couse it curtailed the English summer that year. In the last week of August, Jim was working a local stopping train and his van stopped right by Rasputin's office. Hearing Jim's voice, Rasputin came out, looked Jim straight in the eye and said, 'It looks as if you will be back here shortly Smith!' 'No,' said Jim, 'I won't be back here until I wear the foreman's hat.'

'Humph,' said Rasputin, turned on his heel and went into his office. Jim ran into Rasputin on several occasions in the war years, but Rasputin never again spoke to Jim. Incidentally Jim never worked under Rasputin ever again.

Under The Table

The goods guards and the porters were often trying practical jokes on each other. The advantage usually lay with the goods guards because they ranged further and talked with more people, but Jim Smith and Vernon had some success. One morning when there was no-one about they went into the guards' locker room and nailed a kipper to the underside of their table.

Now, one of the goods guards was detailed to wash out the guards' room each Saturday morning. Some pulled out the tables and chairs to do this - and others didn't. So Jim and Vernon were genuinely surprised and delighted when a month later the table was put out on to the platform, and bits of kipper and a lot of white maggots fell on to the platform. It was wonderful how many people had (in hindsight) smelled 'something funny' in the guards' room.

Rail motor car at Dawlish 1910s.

Some Gets In Your Eyes

The toilets at Rasputin's station were very deep. From the doors to the seats was about seven feet, therefore, anyone using the seats was well away from the doors. There were four of them and there was a gap of nine inches under each door and the internal dividing walls. Jim Smith was sitting on the throne one day when Mac, the station joker, got a piece of dry cotton waste (used for cleaning locomotives), lit it and pushed it just under the door where it was well out of Jim's reach.

Jim came out in a great hurry, kicking the smoking waste into the urinal gutter, and coughing and spluttering vowed to have his revenge on Mac. The following day he seemed to get his chance, for Mac finished his breakfast, got up and disappeared into the toilets. Jim got his piece of cotton waste, lit it, walked into the toilets and pushed it gently under the toilet door. He then busied himself oiling barrows and waiting results. What happened next both surprised and delighted Jim. Out rushed Rasputin and Mac, still pulling up their trousers and spluttering and coughing very satisfactorily.

Charlie Books On

At Rasputin's station, eight porters and two shunters shared one small cabin. A booking-on form was supplied daily and the ten men signed themselves on duty under the eye of the foreman.

Rasputin came in one day, examined the signing on sheet, and gave it as his opinion that someone was signing in for more than one man. 'This will have to stop,' he said. The staff were dumbfounded. No such thing had entered their heads. The last man on duty that week was Charlie Davies who came on duty at 4:15. Charlie was a real artist; his pen and ink drawings and his pencil sketches were extremely good. He could sketch free hand or copy with great accuracy.

Now Charlie sat down with a pencil and carefully wrote every man's signature and booked time for the following day. Just after 4:15 the next day Rasputin came into the cabin, carefully examined Charlie's handiwork, expressed pleasure that each man had that day signed for himself only, and ordered that it must stay that way.

Delivery

Frank had the lorry at the parcels office doorway and was stacking the town round on the basis of last in first out. Sheppard's van came alongside and the young fellow who drove it went inside and asked the parcel porter if there was anything for his firm on hand. He often did this for it enabled his firm to get earlier delivery. The parcel porter knew that there was a parcel of about two cubic feet for Sheppard's and he had himself entered it upon Frank's delivery sheet; so he took the parcel back off Frank's lorry, and obtained the driver's signature on the delivery sheet.

There was one thing however that he didn't know. Frank had found a very small parcel for Pollards Engineering, who had their works next to Sheppard's and had tucked it under the string of Sheppard's parcel in order that it might be readily found and not lost. Some four minutes later Frank set off around the town delivering as he went. He was approaching Sheppard's factory at one o'clock; he took his sandwiches out, and went into the Black Horse, ordered a pint of bitter, and sat down and ate his sandwiches and drank his pint. A quarter of an hour later he climbed back into his cab, and went on with his deliveries. He noted that Sheppard's parcel had been signed for, and he searched for the very small parcel for Pollards and could not find it. Now he could well remember that he had slipped it under the string of the Sheppard's parcel so he assumed that it had been overlooked and went to Sheppard's stores depot, explained the position, and expected that it would be handed to him. Instead the store keeper told him, 'Anything we have has been signed for, so it stays here.' In vain Frank asked him to be reasonable. Nothing would move him. He would not permit Frank to examine the latest parcel which he could see on the floor behind him.

Frank walked out and went to Sheppards' office and asked to see the manager. The manager listened to Frank and then to his surprise, supported his storeman and told Frank to leave the man alone. Frank went to the nearest phone box and rang the station and explained the situation. Jim the foreman told him to carry on with his round, but not to return to the station. An hour later, having completed his deliveries, Frank returned to Sheppards and parked outside. He was soon joined by Jim the foreman, a man six-foot-two-inches in height and of powerful build. With him was another man whom Frank knew as the district railway detective.

They went into Sheppards' stores dept. Frank left it to the detective who endeavoured to persuade the store keeper to allow them to look at the parcel which was still on the floor at the rear of the store. Nothing stirred him, so the "tec ." went to the office and returned with the manager. He would do nothing, and when asked why, he said, 'Your man came to my office drunk, and demanded that I give up a parcel which we have never received.'

Bristol Canons Marsh goods depot. Date not known. It formed part of the Bristol Docks railway system.

Now Frank had never been drunk in his life, and hotly denied it. The manager said, 'His lorry was parked outside the Black Horse for a long time lunchtime.' Frank protested that he had only had one pint with his sandwiches and that the landlord of the Black Horse would be able to vouch for him. Jim told the "tec." and the Sheppards manager that he didn't need anybody to vouch for Frank. He had known him throughout his railway career and had never known him to fail in his duty or to tell a lie. Now the manager ordered them all out. They turned as if to walk towards the door then Jim brushed the manager to one side as if he were a feather, lifted the counter flap and shoved the storekeeper out of the way. He picked up the parcel, dumped it on the counter, turned it over and there under the string was the little parcel for Pollards Engineering. The "tec." showed it to the manager and made noises about charges of theft.

Frank picked up the parcel and his delivery sheet and went next door to Pollards. He put the parcel on their stores counter and said, 'Sign here please.' The storeman signed the sheet and said, 'About time too. We have been waiting all day for this!'

The First Diesels

Round about 1938 the Great Western started to build a series of diesel railcars. The first fifteen or so were designed to run as single units only, and were beautifully streamlined. Later there were several variants, but some of the originals were put into service between Bristol and Weymouth and Chippenham. The G.W.R. found it necessary to issue a warning of the near silent and high speed approach of these vehicles, and we learned to be very wary of them.

The trouble was that other noises would drown the sound of their approach even when we were listening for them. This is what happened to me.

I was pushing a two wheeled trolley over the Barrow crossing with a ten gallon empty oil drum on it, and the noise of the bouncing empty drum drowned the approach of the diesel. It struck the two wheeler which I was pushing ahead of me and knocked it out of my hands. I fell to the ground though quite unhurt and the diesel was already gone. I picked up the two wheeler and the oil drum, neither of which was damaged, and got on with what I was doing. It was five minutes later that I got the 'shakes'. There was no report of any damage to the diesel.

Lawrence Hill Station - Bristol, with a passenger train standing on the down relief line. 1900s.

Clifton Down Station, Bristol - pre-World War I. The station has a severe curve and was built with an enormous amount of iron cast work.

Slips

The slip coach was much used by the Great Western Railway, but whether it was used elsewhere is beyond my knowledge. It was a method of detaching coaches from a train without the train stopping. Slip sections could be of one, two or three coaches and a train could carry a maximum of three slip portions. A typical example would be from London. Third slip detached for Westbury, serving the Weymouth line; second slip detached for Taunton, serving the Minehead branch and first slip detached Newton Abbot, serving the Torbay line. The slip was usually attached to a train from some other area to complete its journey, i.e. the Weymouth slip would be attached at Westbury to a train from Bristol. The advantage lay in the fact that by the time the slip came to a stand in Westbury station, the main train was approaching Frome.

Each slip section had a separate guard and his van was completely shut off from the rest of the train. The slipping apparatus inside the van was extremely simple, consisting of a lever like a miniature signal-box lever, a brass quadrant on which it operated, and an extra vacuum gauge. There was also, of course, a normal hand-brake. The hook of a slip section was hinged and the lever inside the van released the lock on that hinge when it was pulled, and also partially applied the brake. The coupling then fell from the hook and the two portions parted. The guard then pushed the lever back to the midway position and the vacuum brake came off and allowed the slip portion to run on under its own momentum. By means of a system of storage tanks, the vacuum brake could be applied and released twice more. But many of the old-time slip guards could bring their charge to a stand exactly where required by means of the hand brake alone, and many preferred to do it this way, thus giving their passengers a much smoother stop. The extra vacuum gauge was to show the state of affairs in the storage tanks.

Before a slip section was rigged for use, adaptors had to be placed between the respective steam and vacuum pipes, so that these could remain closed to the atmosphere even when the pipes themselves had parted. Another refinement called for in slip coach working was the outer distant signal. At places where slipping was regularly carried out, these signals were erected well in rear of the ordinary distant signal and locked the inner distant signal on the off position. In the early 1930s the completion of the avoiding lines at Westbury and Frome forced a rethink on the Weymouth line slips. It was then arranged for the slip to be stopped short of the crossover road at Heywood Road Junction, where the Westbury pilot engine picked it up, and brought it into the station. It is said that an old-time porter at Westbury, if he had been short of tips, would take a passenger and his bags off the slip portion at one platform, and put him or her in the main train at the next platform, and having obtained his tip would disappear when the slip was shunted on behind.

There was a rather complicated maneouvre carried out with a slip coach off the 7:55 Paddington to Pembroke Dock train. An engine and two or three coaches worked from Temple Meads to North Filton platform with office workers of the aircraft works. The signal-box at North Filton platform by the way, was Filton West Junction. When the office workers had been detrained, the train was then propelled to Stoke Gifford. Here for the next hour or so it was in everyone's way and was shunted from one side to the other. Eventually the 7:55 Paddington would come tearing down the main line and the slip coach could be seen approaching the East home signal. The local train was then propelled to the East home signal and attached to the slip. Then off it went calling at all stations from Filton Junction to Weston-Super-Mare. Slip coaches disappeared with nationalisation.

The "Aberdeen"

Some of the routes worked by the railways in pre-war days would seem rather odd today. For instance, the daily Wolverhampton to Weymouth service via Birmingham (Snow Hill), Oxford, Swindon, and Westbury. An even greater oddity was the "Aberdeen" which ran from Westbury to Swindon via Melksham. At least it was only over this stretch that it had the title, as far as I know. It consisted of a brake-compo and a van for Glasgow and a brake-compo for Aberdeen. Sometimes there was an additional van for Aberdeen.

It started each day from Penzance at eleven in the morning, attached to the Paddington Express. At tea-time (just before five) it had reached Westbury and was there detached. At twenty-past-five it became, for a short time, a train in its own right, and ran to Swindon. Here it was attached to the Swindon to York train and ran via Banbury to the LNER. After that we had no knowledge of its progress, but continued to load our Newcastle, Edinburgh, and Dundee parcels into its van, and of course the Glasgow van was well-loaded every night. Another oddity about it - its balancing vehicles did not reach Penzance by the same route. Where I was stationed we did not see them at all when westward bound.

Lost Token

On single lines of railway there are many methods in use to prevent trains colliding head on by ensuring that only one train is present in the section at a time. Of these the best is probably the single line token. This is a small object about eight inches long with a key piece at one end and a flat plate at the other, bearing the names of the two stations between which the token is in use. No driver may enter the single line without being in possession of a token. As only one token can be obtained from the two machines at any one time, the system is as nearly foolproof as man can make it. If two trains are to follow one another through the same section, the first token must be put into the machine at the far end before another token can be drawn for the second train. The section between Devizes and Patney and Chirton was one such worked by these machines. In order to make sure a wrong token is not taken into a section, the token for neighbouring sections are painted different colours, usually yellow, blue, red or green, though I have seen white ones. The Patney - Devizes token was blue. The tokens are carried in a metal ring and secured by a spring.

One afternoon, many years ago, the fireman of a down train exchanged tokens with the Devizes signalman handing him the ring carrier. The signalman immediately said, 'Where's the token, this carrier is empty.' They searched the engine but no trace of the token could be found. Enquiries at Patney signal-box concluded that the driver had certainly received a token. The two signalmen then tried to extract a token, but neither could succeed, proving that there was a token missing.

There was no alternative but to open up pilot working, which is the emergency method of operation by which an appointed pilotman represents the token and operates in roughly the same way. The following day the line was worked in this way and every available man was out searching the track for the missing token. It was not found, so the fact of it being missing was entered in the duty notices, and the signal linesman was authorised to adjust the token machine so as to allow normal working to be resumed. The daily notices continued to contain news of the loss of the token and then eventually transferred to the monthly and national notices. Everyone gave up the idea of ever finding the token and autumn came.

Two boys in one of the local villages were great friends. They were both 12 and they both loved the outdoors so they often went miles together. Fred was a fishing fanatic, while Jim was interested in all wildlife, but particularly birds. Fred settled down by the canal and Jim climbed a tree with his binoculars. The grass had been cropped short by a flock of sheep and Jim could see the rabbits under the opposite hedgerow. A magpie was pecking at something shiny quite near the rabbits. Jim idly wondered what could be shiny, for any metal out in the open for a few days would be rusty; there had been so much rain.

The magpie flew away. Jim watched a hawk hovering. It took no notice of

Single-line electric token. See The Lost Token.

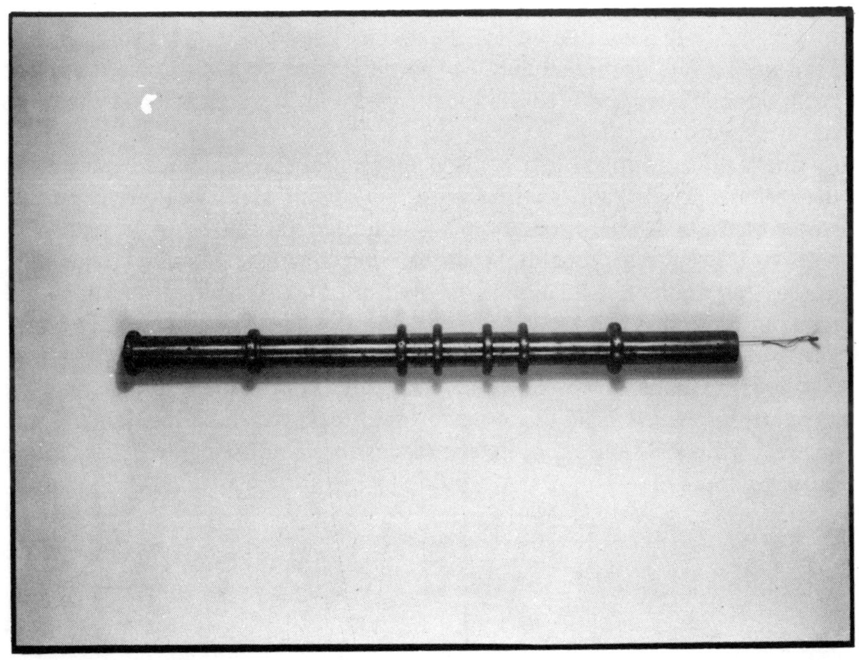

Single-line staff. It had the same uses as a single line token but was of an older pattern for a different type of machine.

the shiny object but swooped rapidly and grabbed a field mouse, and flew off with it. Immediately the magpie returned and turned the metal object over, dancing away as it overbalanced. Jim began to be interested in the magpie's find, started over and eventually picked it up. Stamped into the flat end were the words Devizes, Patney and Chirton. The other end was like a large key and there were flecks of blue paint left on it. Jim went back and showed it to Fred. They agreed it was a queer looking object, but neither knew what it was. 'Throw it away,' said Fred, but curiosity made Jim put it back into his pocket. They realised dusk was falling and left the canal and started towards home. They passed a man they both knew, though he lived in the next village. 'Night, Mr Wells,' they said. 'Night boys,' said Jim Wells. After they had passed, something made Jim Wells look back at them and he saw the token protruding from his young namesake's pocket. He called out, 'Here, lad. What's thee got in thy pocket.'

'Nothing,' said Jim and started to run. Jim Wells called after him. 'Don't mean thee no harm young un, but that might be valuable, and dangerous.' He had to shout and that did not reassure young Jim who ran all the way home and flopped into a chair.

Jim Wells arrived one minute later, and was faced by the boy's father who was a bit annoyed at his boy's state of near collapse. Jim Wells carefully explained the position and the importance of the token. 'Then where is this token,' said the other man. 'Jim hasn't got it.' The two men tackled the boy who would only deny that he had the token. They asked if he had given it to Fred but he said no. Eventually Jim admitted that he had thrown it into the roadside soon after Jim Wells had challenged him. It was now too late to see to recover the token.

Jim Wells rang up his district inspector on the nearest public telephone and then fetched a hurricane lantern from a railway hut which was very close, and stayed on the spot where young Jim had indicated for the rest of the night. His wife had been told roughly what had happened and walked over with sandwiches and coffee for him and stayed until ten o'clock. Just after six the next morning, one of his mates arrived, and Jim Wells went home to bed. He got up at dinner-time and there came a knock at the front door. Standing there was his district inspector. 'Come in,' said Jim. 'How is the search going?' 'We have just succeeded,' said the inspector, 'where do you think we found it?' and answering his own question, 'in the biggest bunch of stinging nettles for 50 miles around.'

The Burnham Excursion

It was on August Bank Holiday 1939 that the railway ran an excursion from (I believe) Salisbury to Burnham. It was not expected to have too great an appeal, for it consisted only of a Southern "set", two brake seconds and a "compo". But it was a very fine day, and perhaps Burnham had not been featured in that area before.

Enough passengers for two such trains turned up. Around tea-time on that day I was sent to Highbridge to bring this excursion back to Bristol, where some other guard would relieve me. I ate my meal at Highbridge, and as I finished, the train ran in on to the down platform. The Somerset and Dorset engine was released and the Western engine attached. I looked in the front van. It was a seething mass of people, and although the weather had cooled somewhat, the heat in that van was extraordinary. Now these vans had solid wooden sliding doors and the end windows were a fixture. Only the guard's doors had drop-down windows, so the ventilation was extremely poor.

I foresaw that the passengers might try to open the sliding doors to get air, which would have been very dangerous, so I locked them on both sides. People were standing in the passenger compartments and sitting on each other's laps. The rear van was in the same state as the front one. I had to force my way in with my gear. I had a word with the Station Master, 'Bristol must provide extra coaches,' I said. He agreed to send the message on, but both he and I had grave doubts about getting extras on a Bank Holiday evening.

I locked the sliding doors on the rear van and we set off. As we left Highbridge I was relieved to hear the passengers in the front van singing. We had a very poor run stopping frequently for signals. I was hoping we did not stop in a station, so I was pleased to travel main line instead of via the Weston-super-Mare loop. My luck ran out at Yatton; we stopped in the platform and as the signal was pulled off, the passengers jumped out, and both men and women ran to the toilets. The driver started the train without looking back again. I was therefore obliged to apply the vacuum setter and stop it. The original passengers came back to the train - relieved - but more and more left it.

About seven minutes was lost trying to get everyone aboard again, while the signalman behind us was tearing his hair (well, almost!). Eventually we got away again, and the delays resulted in us getting a through run to Temple Meads. There was no hope there of getting extra coaches. I saw the inspector, told him of the state of the train, and advised him if there were no strengthening coaches, to get the train out of the station as quickly as he could. This is the way a day-out went in 1939.

Burnham has, of course, no railway today so this could possibly have been among the last excursion trains to run there.

Wartime

Signs of War

In August 1939 the clouds of war were gathering, but I think many of us believed that somehow it would be prevented at the last moment. During the fateful week preceding the declaration of war, I was working daily to Portishead. The old station was then in use, right under the shadow of the electricity generating station. This old station had the peculiarity of a pub on the platform. I only came across two others like it.

On the Monday of that week came the first sign. A banana boat which had been laid up there for a very long time was raising steam. On Tuesday she had sailed. She was part of the scenery and her absence was conspicuous. On the Wednesday I heard voices from an unfamiliar source and discovered that men were gathered on the roof of the generating station. On the Thursday there were machine-guns mounted there. I was now certain that this time it was the 'real thing' and the dread of war at that time was worse than any experience after it started. I know that many among my generation felt like that. On Saturday evening I went to Portishead for a look round the little town and a couple of pints of beer. On the way back to Bristol there were no lights on the train and I went to complain to the guard. He told me that he had orders to show no lights and none would be switched on. Had war been declared? Not that he knew.

But it happened next day. Chamberlain had us glued to the radio while he announced that we were at war with Germany. Many of us actually felt relief that at last we knew where we were.

The Derailment

The war years could be pretty grim for a shunter. Long hours, dirty work and an element of danger. No let-up during working hours meant utter weariness. One morning I managed to get the branch passenger derailed. I wasn't soley to blame but I let that slip and pleaded guilty. My boss at this depot was a complete railwayman - far removed from the bungling amateurs who filled some station masters' jobs.

Some three weeks after the derailment our boss came in while we were at breakfast and told me that he had a free ticket sent for me to go to Bristol for a disciplinary hearing in connection with the derailment. Having already pleaded guilty I figured they couldn't do very much to me so I said, 'Well isn't that nice of them. At last I'll get a day off!'

'You can forget that,' said the boss. 'You are not going. I've told Bristol I can't spare you, and that I have dealt with you severely. Don't do it again!'

Winter 1939-40

The winter of 1939-40 was very severe in Britain. For the troops in France it must have been worse, but it gave the railwaymen of Britain many a headache. The worst came at one weekend. All day on the Sunday the rain came down steadily and saturated everything. Then, very suddenly, came the frost. The temperature went way down and the millions of rain droplets turned immediately to ice. All night, Sunday - Monday, could be heard the crashing of tree branches overloaded with the tons of ice. The wires of the telephone system snapped under the load, or pulled the poles over.

I went to work at Devizes station at six in the morning, having no idea how severe was the effect of the icing. Now Devizes was on top of the downs and was a very cold spot. The signal-box contained two tokens for the lower section, one to Seend which was the normal section, and one to Holt junction for use on nights, when Seend was switched out. The morning signalman rang his bell to switch Seend in, but nothing happened. He tried to get Seend on the telephone but did not succeed. He was about to put the phone back on the hook when a voice asked plaintively, 'That you Bert? Why don't you answer my bell?' Having established a communication, however unsatisfactory, they tried to switch in and failed; neither of them could get a token out.

Having been called to the signal-box by the signalman, I suggested they switch back out, and we could then use the night token. They tried this, but it proved impossible. We were faced with opening pilot working. We called many taxis on the GPO telephone but could get only one answer, and this man refused to turn out. Other than the signalman I was the senior man on duty, for the foreman lived a long way off and the journey turned out to be incredibly difficult. It seemed I would have to walk through the section to inaugurate the pilot working. Then the ganger suggested that I use their trolley, and he would spare two of his men to help it through the section. I was afraid that the trolley might run away with us on the very steep gradient known as Cane Hill, leading from Devizes to Seend. So we took a brake stick to counteract this possibility. We need not have bothered, the ice lay on top of the rail about three-eighths of an inch thick and we had to scoot the trolley all down Cane Hill.

We got to Bromham Halt and delivered forms to the porter there and obtained his signature acknowledging the pilot working. Here we put the trolley aside, and I left the engineers and walked in alone to Seend. I slipped and fell many times, for the ice was everywhere and there was no safe footing anywhere. When I arrived at Seend box and exchanged pilot working forms with the signalman, there was a train waiting to proceed. The Seend-Holt Junction staff was in working order. The signalman had agreed to listen at five minute intervals on the telephone, for although they could speak to each other, neither bell would ring. I showed myself to the waiting driver, and ordered him to proceed, and awaited the following train.

The difficulty I had was in answering the driver's very proper questions regarding the signalling at the opposite end of the section. I had to use the formula, 'When I left, the signalman was - etc., but an attempt is being made to do so and so.' The second train drew in and I went aboard the engine. Until now I had imagined that the conditions were due mainly to the height of Devizes above sea level, but the driver of this train was able to inform me that there was scarcely a section in the West of England without some communication problem. This dashed our hopes of getting a linesman, for he would obviously be busy on more important sections. It was in fact three days before he could rectify our faulty apparatus.

We set off back towards Devizes. We had one bit of luck. The trolley, and later the first train, had dispersed the ice from the rail and we had a couple of hand signalmen on duty at Devizes, for the signal wires were frozen solid. When I arrived there I found that the foreman was acting as the pilotman on the Devizes-Patney section, for although there was still communication here, the telegraph wires were leaning at crazy angles and failure was expected at any time. This went on as I said for three days and two nights during which time I learned more about pilotman's duties than many men do in a lifetime. In the beginning I had to rely on my very knowledgable signalman for I was rather ignorant of the rules in the matter. By the end of the spell I had these rules word perfect. It was the longest spell of pilot working I ever personally came across.

Fire

The Focke Wolfe 190 came over the country station just as the local freight train was shunting the yard, and in broad daylight it dropped a packet of incendiary bombs and disappeared. The siren sounded at that moment. There were five petrol tanks on the siding and one which was standing with its vents open, caught fire.

Percy the guard of the train called the driver back and managed to attach the string of tanks, and detach the last two which were O.K. He sent the driver forward with the blazing tank on the rear of the string of wagons and stopped him when they were well clear of the depot. He now tried to detach the burning tank in order to isolate it, but the heat was too great. He couldn't get close enough. There was only one thing he could do. He detached the burning tank and one other, threw down the hand brake and signalled the driver to go ahead with the remaining tank and the string of other wagons.

Percy ran after them until he thought the distance rendered it safe, then sat down on a pile of sleepers to recover. Of course the fire brigade had been sent for while this was happening, and they arrived very promptly, in fact they were quick enough to save the other tank from burning or exploding. We, at Percy's home depot, only found out about this because of his annoyance with some stupid clerk at a safe office in Reading, who wrote twice to Percy demanding to know why he had detached two tanks when only one was burning.

Dunkirk

The police came to the door just after midnight. Their knocking, though discreet, nevertheless alarmed my old landlady. The landlord went to the door then fetched me. I had heard someone say police, and since it was a licenced premises I had presumed it would be the landlord they wanted. I slipped into a dressing gown and went down to the private bar. The constable said to me, 'You are to go to the railway station and open everything up and you will get further orders then.'

When I arrived at the station (Devizes, Wilts - now deserted) I was met by three army officers; the senior, swearing me to secrecy. I opened the waiting room and let them in to use it as an office and, with a bit of luck, the porter arrived at the moment and I told him to get a fire going for them and also one in the porters' room for us. A section of men arrived with a sergeant and the colonel took me and the sergeant into the signal-box to consult with the signalman. Then I heard the news of Dunkirk, for we were to receive train loads of the men who had been rescued from the beaches.

In Devizes at that time was the Wiltshire regiment's barracks and also a large training and transit camp, then unfinished. The colonel required that the trains should be brought direct to the up platform although they were coming from the London direction - that is they were down trains. Patney and Chirton signal-box was given instructions to give to the drivers, then between two and three in the morning I clamped and padlocked the down facing points, and the up catch point, and hand-signalled the first train into the platform.

The army section under the sergeant, the porter, the two lieutenants and myself set about getting the men out into the road, where the lorries were waiting to take them to camp. What I write now is what I saw. The trains were full of uneaten food, the men were often difficult to rouse, and I saw men fall asleep while walking down the train corridors. But when roused the first thing they did was to grab their rifle; and they all had their rifles. Lined up for loading into the lorries, some dropped in the road asleep.

When we had unloaded the men, we searched the train. We did find a few rifles and many other more personal things and small equipment, and all this was stored in the waiting room. The uneaten food was left where it was, the men had obviously been much too tired to eat. Just as we finished searching the first train the foreman arrived. He had had to ride from Westbury by road. He walked past me into a centre gangwayed vehicle. We were calling to one another as we found different things, 'I've found a small pack.'

'I've got a great coat,' and then the foreman, 'I've found a tommy.' A youngster was there - no more than seventeen years old - sound asleep. Everything happened at once. The young man woke and screamed and grabbed at his rifle. I shoved the foreman to one side and grabbed his left hand which had just reached the rifle. 'You are alright young'un. You are home,' I said. He looked at me and said, 'Who are you?' I said, 'I'm nobody but you are in Britain and safe. He broke down and cried, and the tension was broken.

The first train departed and we had a cup of tea and a rest. The colonel came into the porters' room, ignored the foreman, much to his chagrin and informed me that the second train had passed Pewsey. I introduced the foreman saying I was no longer in charge. Five of these specials arrived before I was relieved at two in the afternoon. After the daily service started, things got much more complicated, but we muddled through. We were using the back platform for uptrains, and ordinary downtrains were using their own platform while the specials used the up platforms. This was the only platform with direct access to the road.

Everyone was soon tired out, but the men we were working for were in far worse plight and the army brewed gallons of tea and there was plenty to eat. Though it was arranged that I would book on again at midnight we had no more specials from Dunkirk. About a week later (my memory is not accurate with this detail) we had two specials from the St Valery evacuation. The first of these was British troops, but the second was French. They left all their gear aboard the train which was under guard from our men. We were all sworn to secrecy about the train's destination which at the time was absurd for we had no idea where it was going.

The French soldiers were taken to the camp and fed, and they cleaned up and were brought back to the station. By this time we had somehow discovered that they were being taken to Southampton for return to France. Whether this actually happened I do not know, but it was my impression that those men would rather have stayed in Britain. What was obvious was that our army chiefs feared they might mutiny if they were told, and they were very relieved when the train left. I vaguely felt that we had done a dirty trick on the young Frenchmen.

A Quart in a Pint Pot

In 1939 the GWR brought out the latest type of its pre-war diesel cars. They were painted in the old chocolate and cream livery and had numbers in the middle thirties. Unlike the earlier types, they were not very well streamlined and were built to run in pairs, but they had an experimental buffet (never used), and a van, and two driving compartments, so the passenger accommodation was very limited.

Before they had been in use very long they had an ordinary coach added between the two units and this doubled the seating capacity. This triple set came into use between Bristol and Weymouth. For some reason, which I could never fathom, they could not be relied upon to operate the track circuits. That is to say they were not to be relied upon to work the several electrical devices which should have indicated their presence to the signalman.

One morning just after the departure of this unit I had gone to the signal-box in connection with a message and noted that the diesel was indicated on the diagram as approaching the advanced starting signal, which was way out of sight around the bend. The indicator lights went out, and the signalman put the advanced starter back to danger, and I left the signal-box and started off down the platform. I had just reached the other end of the platform when the guard of the diesel unit came puffing up and said that the signal had been put back before they had got to it, whereas I had seen for myself that the lights had gone out before the signal was replaced at danger.

I telephoned the signalman who was able to pull the signal off again, then had to leave it off until he got the 'train out of section signal' from the box in advance. During this time, rules prohibited him from using the starting signal in the station which stopped us shunting for quite some time.

This procedure had to be followed each day from then on. The unit used to return to Bristol in the early afternoon, and one day we had a crowd of about a hundred waiting to board it and I knew very well that they would not all get aboard, for it would arrive fairly well loaded and the accommodation was very limited. But this day when it ran in, it was already packed tight, and obviously nobody was going to be able to join it. Our intending passengers were furious, for the next train was a considerable time later. But the worst was yet to come. The examiner found a broken spring on the middle coach and put a red no-go card on it. We unloaded the eighty or so passengers who were sitting and standing in the coach and detached the damaged vehicle.

The passengers now wanted blood. We could not even replace the damaged vehicle; there were no coach available. As I was the one who was actually detaching the vehicle, I came in for more than my share of the 'blame', yet my sympathies lay entirely with the passengers. So the unit left with about eighty less passengers than it arrived with. Only the British would have put with it, any other nation would have burned the station down.

Revenge is not always sweet

Some of the things that happened years ago and particularly in war-time would not be condoned today and would be frowned upon. Nevertheless they happened, and some had tinges of humour.

Jack Flint worked as a shunter in a fairly large marshalling yard on the outskirts of a large city. The yard had a large farm just the other side of the downside fence. Only two miles away was a nationally important aircraft works so it really was a target area. One night the air raid sirens sounded and the men picked up their food bags and started off towards the shelter. Jack was trailing along last as usual. He would not allow 'Jerry' to make him rush.

The first aircraft appeared almost immediately. The anti-aircraft batteries and their searchlights opened up. Jack looked up and saw a Heinkel trapped in the searchlights and cursed it. Then it dropped its main load of bombs. The first dropped on the airport perimeter and the next four were nearer and nearer to Jack. Then the last one dropped on the farm - on the huge manure heap. Many tons of manure went flying up into the air and about a hundredweight dropped on Jack. It knocked the breath completely out of him and he came round gasping and what he swallowed was not nice to tell. He was otherwise quite uninjured but the rest of his mates came to find him, and then perhaps wished they hadn't for Jack went down into the shelter completely covered in manure.

His language was unbelievable. His mates who knew he had a choice turn of phrase could scarcely believe the extent of his vocabulary. Luckily there was a water supply in the shelter and Jack was able to clean off a bit. All his mates held their noses and kept to the far corner away from him. Jack was saying what he would do to that Jerry pilot if only he could get hold of him; suffice it to say that his death would have been extremely painful. Half-an-hour later the all clear sounded and everyone except Jack came from the shelter and got on with their work. Jack went up the hill to his home to get cleaned up, and was still so plastered in muck that, whilst he stripped and washed, his wife locked him in the scullery for an hour and looked out all clean clothes for him. For many weeks after that the banter which Jack had to take was continuous and cruel. The train crews calling at the yard got to know about it, and because Jack was such a well-known and well-liked character, the story was known far and wide.

The other half of the story took place a year later. Again the sirens sounded the alarm and the ack-ack opened up. This time Jack was at home and he watched events from the metal shelter in the garden; he saw an aircraft catch fire and he came up out of the shelter and watched it. It was a moonlit night, but with some cloud. Jack saw that the plane on fire was a Messerschmitt 109, a single seater, and then he saw the parachute open and watched where it went. He could tell that it was coming down to the north-east of him. He went indoors and picked up his Winchester rifle and fixed the bayonet upon it for he was a member of the home-guard. He shouted to his wife where he was going and ran up the road and across the branch rail-track. He came to the big spinney and crept quietly through, but saw no one, and when he paused he heard none, though he listened intently.

He crossed a sixty acres field and then looked down into the little valley and saw the parachute. He could not however see the pilot. The moon went behind the cloud and he crossed the little valley whilst it did so, and came to the Badgers Holt coppice. He thought he heard movement and froze. He heard it again and moved towards it, then froze again. At that moment a certain smell came to Jack and he realised he was close to farmer Ambrose Slater's church ground and Ambrose had recently bought the most modern of muck spreaders, as a matter of fact Ambrose had spread 'church ground' that very afternoon.

Little evil thoughts came into Jack's head, but first he had to find his jerry pilot. He was standing stock still, when the pilot, in stepping forward, fell over a mound of earth from one of the badger's many excavations. He fell upon his face and as he went to rise Jack's bayonet touched the back of his neck and Jack's voice said, 'Now thee bide there a minute and get thee breath back.' He lay there. 'Right,' said Jack, 'let's see if thee's got a revolver, and bending over him discovered that he had and relieved him of it.

'Now,' said Jack, putting the revolver in his jacket pocket, 'we'll go for a nice country walk.' They went up the bank from Badger's Holt coppice and through the wire fence into 'church ground'. The German appeared reluctant to move so Jack gave him a none too gentle prod with his bayonet and to his delight the German slipped to his hands and knees. He prodded him upright again and they sloughed on across the field.

The fact that he was getting really mucky himself, did not worry Jack. He kept the prisoner going at a good pace and had the satisfaction of having him fall on his face twice. They went down beside Ambrose Slater's duck pond where he fell onto his knees again, and then on through Ambrose's farm yard where the slurry was three inches deep. The prisoner turned to protest but Jack prodded him on. Eventually they came out into the village street and Jack marched the prisoner up the garden of the local police station, and banged upon the door.

Constable Felton opened the door, smelled the two of them, recognised Jack and said, 'Who the heck have you got there Jack.' The prisoner spoke for the first time. He had seen the police helmet hanging in the hall. He said, 'Please, you are polizei?' The officer admitted it. The prisoner said, 'Then please you take me away from this very fierce old man, he pokes me much with that bayonet.' Jack handed over the prisoner and the revolver, and the constable said, 'Go and clean up and come back after breakfast for questioning.'

Jack came back to the station at about nine o'clock, the constable was present and introduced Jack to his inspector. There was another man sitting in a chair in the office, he was dressed in old grey trousers and blue striped shirt and a brown pullover; he looked as if he might have been a local carpenter or farm labourer. 'Who is he?' asked Jack pointing.

'You don't know,' said the inspector, 'why he is your prisoner of last night. We had to fix him up with what togs we could get, for he was filthy with muck.' Jack looked at the man. He was really seeing him for the first time. He was a very ordinary looking young man, not so tall or so broad shouldered as Jack, and Jack suddenly felt a bit ashamed of the way he had prodded this young fellow for about a mile-and-a-half through the muckiest country he could find.

A Drastic Cure

In 1939-40 a large army camp was under construction at Devizes. Part of the construction involved the loading at Devizes station and haulage of many thousands of tons of gravel. The haulage was done by different firms, many of them just owning one lorry. All the contracts were on a piecework basis and competition between the lorry drivers was intense. When it was necessary to shunt the long siding in order to remove the empties and to put in newly arrived loaded wagons the arguments were fierce. Those who had wagons to be emptied refused to get out in order to allow shunting to start, and those who were waiting for their wagons were very angry. The situation was well nigh impossible. We would attach the engine and then spend much valuable time trying to get men out of the wagons and were roundly abused for doing so. We were of course strictly forbidden to shunt with anyone in the wagons.

One day a driver anxious to get on with his work in order to go home, suggested an answer. It involved breaking rules, and taking a big risk, but we were desperate. We hooked up the string of wagons, warned everybody once, and pulled the 25 wagons forward for shunting. Now, at the London end of Devizes is a fairly long tunnel on top of which incidentally is Devizes Castle. The method of shunting was to use a klaxon horn. A different number of blasts meant: go forward, go back, stop etc. On this day nobody got out of the wagons, they all thought they could make us wait for their convenience. Instead they found themselves in Devizes tunnel, where the fireman immediately put lots of wet coal on the fire, and closed the dampers thus causing an immense cloud of thick black smoke.

The draught of the tunnel carried it back toward the station, totally enclosing the lorry drivers in the wagons. They couldn't even see to jump out. The driver waited until the fire started to clear, then came back into the middle siding. We cut off the first empties then said, 'Anyone who wants to get out has 30 seconds before we send you back into the tunnel for a second dose.' They came out in a hurry still coughing and spitting with their faces black as soot. After that we had no trouble getting them out, nor did we ever tell them more than once again. None of them made any official complaint or we could have been in serious trouble.

In The Dark

The red alert sounded at 22:30 hours and the 'all clear' at 06:10. Around midnight the marshalling yard came under attack, and the crew in the deep shelter counted the bombs. They counted three explosions and two dropped with the great thud that meant penetration without explosion. The morning shift examined the damage, found the craters and the one unexploded bomb in the tracks, and sent for the army bomb disposal squad. They also found the long skid-type marks of a bomb which bounced; picked up its fins, but no trace of the bomb itself could be found. All the available rail staff looked for clues as to its whereabouts. They would not of course have touched it. The bomb disposal squad arrived, loaded the unexploded bomb and took it away. They searched thoroughly for the other, but could not find it. After 24 hours everything went back to normal though the staff were under warning that anything odd must be immediately reported.

During the following night the controller arranged for some 60 empty wagons which had been standing in No. 3 siding to form a special train to one of the great munitions dumps. The pilot engine attached a brake van to the South Wales end and drew the train down the shunting spur, then the engine arrived and was attached and soon in the blackness of the night the special departed.

The three red lights at the rear gradually disappeared up the cutting and the staff resumed their duties. The wagons were required urgently and the control kept in touch with each signal-box in turn, urging the train forward. It was still dark when the train arrived at the junction where it had to be reversed. The control were soon phoning to find out how the reversal was going. The shunting took quite a long time and by the time it was finished there were a couple of parcel trains which had to precede it. 'Oh hell,' said the chief controller to the signalman, they wanted those wagons before daylight.' The two parcel trains passed and then it was time for another special of even greater priority.

The reversed empty special pulled out as dawn was breaking; it was only another half hour to its destination. It drew into the outer yard there, and the pilot engine drew it down the long shunting spur, leaving the train engine. The shunter reversed the points and called the shunting pilot towards the dump entrance. At this point the yard inspector went up the steps into the storage control-cabin as the wagons started to be propelled into the dump. About 15 wagons had passed when he saw the bomb. It was rolling about in the bottom of an otherwise empty wagon. The yard inspector put his head out of the window showed a red light, and blew three long blasts on his whistle. Everything stopped and everybody heard him shout, 'Pull back down the long spur as far and as slowly as possible and then everybody bale out!'

In a very short time the bomb disposal squad arrived, climbed up into the wagon and set about defusing the bomb. When the controller was told about it he realised that had the train arrived in darkness as had been planned, the bomb would have been carried right into the heart of the great munitions dump and the consequences of that could have been disastrous.

Pride Comes Before

My people lived in Southall. It was not my home, for I had left home before they moved there. It was just an example of the way in which the railway service split up families for my father was also a railwayman. During the war, when I was stationed at Yeovil, I could visit my folks on a week-end following the early turn. I would rush through a meal, a wash, and a quick change and get back to the station for a train in mid-afternoon. This would get me to Westbury to connect with the Penzance to Paddington express. At Westbury I waited for the express at the extreme north-end of the platforms, hoping by this means I might find a seat, for I knew that the middle and rear would be packed solid.

There wasn't a seat available on the train as it turned out, but there was room to stand comfortably. There were a couple of young soldiers there, going home on leave and we were soon talking of things of mutual interest. The train sped on through the Wiltshire downlands. We passed Pewsey. Then two girls came forward into the front coach and stood by the open window. They were pretty girls and well dressed. They were very attractive and they knew it. I was gradually frozen out of the conversation as they monopolised the two young "squaddies". I had experienced something like this on other occasions for I was of course in civilian clothes, and it was to say the least, unfashionable for a young man to be in "civies".

The taller of the two girls, when I spoke of something, said,'Well, who asked you?' and looked down her nose at me. I had a thought and turned to the tall girl and advised her to close the window for the next ten minutes. We passed Hungerford. She answered that with me about she needed all the ventilation she could get. We passed Newbury. I retired around the corner near the lavatory door. We passed Thatcham. One of the young soldiers turned to me and said, 'I wonder you don't slap her in the mouth.'

'There is no need for that,' I said. 'Retribution will follow in just three minutes. Just stay away from that open window.'

The fireman lowered the scoop as we hit the water pick-up troughs and in less than 60 seconds had scooped 3,000 gallons of water into the tender.

As I anticipated a couple of 100 gallons were sprayed along the sides of the leading coach in which we were riding. And about 50 gallons came straight into the open window, saturated the two girls, took their breath away, and almost knocked them down. The two young soldiers just burst out laughing at them, and indeed they were in a right mess.

I was sorry for the smaller one, but for the tall one I felt she had got what she deserved. She got into a terrific temper. 'You knew that was going to happen,' she accused, 'but you didn't say so.' 'Yes miss, I knew,' I said, 'but would you have listened?' They took their cases and disappeared into the toilet, and they were still there when we got out at Paddington.

Powderham Trough. The troughs were found at approximately fifty mile intervals on all of the GWR main lines.

Quite an Ordinary Night

The guard of the branch freight went into the signal-box to telephone his train tally to the controller. It was around nine o'clock on a very dark night. There was no sound except the clank of the fireman's shovel as he made up his fire for the next part of the journey home. George the guard was reeling off the numbers of some livestock wagons - '30643, yes that's right,' when there was a sound of footsteps on the box stairs. He took little notice, thinking it might be his driver come to find out how long he might be. So he only looked up when the signalman said, 'On my God!' A German airman stood there. There had been no 'red alert' so it was very surprising indeed. George said into the phone, 'Now listen to this,' and placed the receiver on top of the wooden cabinet containing the phone apparatus. He was standing around the corner from the airman who could not see what he had done with the receiver, for the signal-box was 'L' shaped, quite an oddity among signal-boxes.

The airman spoke to them in German but neither of them understood him. He opened his flying jacket and showed his uniform below, which didn't help any. However, he had made no gesture to harm anyone, in fact he appeared quite conciliatory. He put his hands up and used one of the few English words he appeared to know. 'Surrender.' Then came the tricky bit. Still talking, he put his hands down and unfastened a holster and took out a revolver with his right hand. While the two railwaymen still wondered what he was about, he transferred it to his left hand and offered it, butt first, to the signalman. He took it and indicating the chair by the fireside said, 'Sit down.' The young German understood this well enough and answered an obvious thank you in his own language.

George picked up the control phone again and asked, 'Did you hear all that?' 'Yes,' said control, 'We have rung the area police. Has he got a gun on him?'

'No,' said George,'he has given it to the signalman.'

'Right,' said control, 'stay in the signal-box until the police arrive.' The driver came to see what the hold-up was about and when he found everything under control went back to his engine. A quarter-of-an-hour later the police arrived and the incident was over. It occurs to me that at the time it was such an ordinary event. Only now it has become a story.

Hospital Trains

At about the time that the Second Front opened, the government deployed a large number of hospital trains around the South of England. The ones we received were of LNER stock, fitted with air pressure brakes of which there were very few indeed in Britain at that time. The correct type of locomotive hauled each train, and at strategic points certain vacuum braked engines were fitted with brakes adaptors so that they could assist such trains if required. To us, who had no specialist knowledge, they appeared to be extremely well-equipped.

Their operating theatre had completely seperate emergency lighting equipment, and a separate boiler room for heating and sterilising. They had dining room and kitchens and doctors' sleeping berths. However their patient accommodation appeared very limited. How many of them there were I do not know, but some were transferred to the Southern via Salisbury and some via Yeovil.

It is probable that other routes were also used. They were dispersed in sidings at small wayside stations, strategically placed to get to the ports which were expected to be used. I only ever saw two of them again, one was carrying young Americans who appeared to be mainly of their engineers regiment. The other carried mainly young Germans, although I thought I saw Americans also on the same train. Perhaps my memory faults me here. It was a long time ago.

Closer Than You Think

The 6:10 pm Weymouth pulled into Yeovil station and the shunter went up to speak to its driver. He had a 63XX class engine (a 2-6-0 tender) and the driver was rather excited. 'A Jerry aircraft has been chasing us,' he said. 'I think he hit one of the coaches.

'Yes,' said the shunter, 'he did, but nobody is hurt, just a hole or two in the lavatory tank.' The driver went on talking and the shunter could not get a word in edgeways. 'We stayed in Grinscone Tunnel,' said the driver, 'because it was a fighter plane and he was sure to be getting short on fuel and sure enough we didn't see him again.' The shunter got his word in while he could. 'If I were you,' he said, 'I would take water here.'

'What for?' said the driver, 'we can get to Westbury easily with this engine.'

'I think not,' said the shunter, 'take a look at your tender this (the fireman's) side.' The driver crossed the footplate and looked long and hard at the dead straight row of holes along the side of the tender which were leaking water at a considerable rate. 'Phew,' he whistled and set about blocking the holes with corks and bits of rag (a steam engine driver always carried corks for use on lubricating studs). As his fireman swung the water crane and started to fill up, he grinned at the shunter and said, 'It's a good job we didn't know it was that close or I would need clean trousers now.'

The Heaviest Train

About a year before the attack on Europe, and while supplies were being built up for its prosecution, Yeovil Pen Mill was sent the largest and most powerful locomotive it ever had, a 63 class D tender locomotive. This was to enable us to assist heavier trains up the Evershot bank. For a while it rendered excellent service, and allowed us to keep the very small yard free of down line traffic.

Then one evening a train load of "AFVs" arrived of a weight no-one ever expected. Oh yes "AFVs" are armoured fighting vehicles and could be tanks, armoured personnel carriers, or self-propelled guns. My foreman looked at the load of this terrifically heavy train, and said to me, 'Even the D class banker won't be enough for this lot.' When I had studied the load, I told him 'Even three engines won't do it. We will need four. But we are not allowed to bank in the rear with a tender engine attached to tank engines, nor are we allowed to bank with three engines at the rear.' So we decided that we must attach the 63XX class engine between the train engine and the train itself. In any case the driver of the train engine decided he would need the assistant engine through to Weymouth, in order to brake it down into Weymouth yard.

In the meantime our own smaller class C tank engine, which was the proper banker, was sent on to Yetminster. Now we had to wait for the Hendford freight and for the head shunter to shunt that train and release the engine. This was then sent to Yetminster, and attached to the engine already there. This engine was a class A tank and was permitted to assist, coupled to the C class.

Now the main train could leave Yeovil, and without stopping, proceed to pass Yetminster, where the two tank engines coupled together, came up behind, overtook it, and pushed it, though unattached, through to Evershot, where they left it and returned to Yeovil.

Without any doubt this was the heaviest train ever to climb Evershot bank.

The Boat Train

There was something magical about that Saturday night. I was on duty at Yeovil, with only the foreman and the signalman. Between ten o'clock and nearly midnight we had worked very hard to clear the shunting in the yard, and then at midnight we had dismissed the pilot to go to Yetminster to act as banker.

We went into the cabin to get our supper and to wait. Two experienced railwaymen wanted to watch a train go by. We had seen them all. Trains carrying royalty, Eisenhower, the General Staff, troops, prisoners, wounded, tanks and supplies, but this one was different. This one was especially ours. Presently, the phone bell in the box outside rang twice. It was the signalman's tip to us that she was coming.

In the quiet night we heard her steaming softly round the curves from Marston Magna and she ran through the platform just as quietly, while we stood silent atop the cabin steps. Under the Sherborne Road bridge she went, and slid round the bend past the cattle pens, and then in answer to the gradient, the driver opened her throttle and she pulled away with a full-throated roar, and in two more minutes was out of hearing range. Yet all down the tracks men like us stood to watch her go by.

We knew we were watching history with thankful hearts. She represented the end of an experience and the coming of a better time. It was the first running of the Channel Islands Boat Express from Paddington to Weymouth, after the liberation of the Islands.

Left to right - fireman, driver, guard. Post Second War.

GWR goods guard in van Nov 1940.

Post War Tales

Shepton Bank

The incline between Wells East Somerset and Shepton Mallet was one of the steepest on the Great Western Railway having a bit of 1 in 43 which is very steep for a steel wheel on a steel rail.

Our main freight locomotive was the 22XX class tender engine of 0-6-0 wheel formation. GWR locomotives were classified in tractive effort from A (the weakest) to E. The 22XX class were B category. The full load for the section was 12 class I (coal or similar) wagons. Soon after the war the standard coal wagon became a 16 tonner, so the loco could only haul eight of these, full loaded, up the bank, and what a struggle it was to do even that!

We were mainly concerned with hauling stone from Cheddar and these were loads which punished the engines most. Leaving Wells East Somerset there was about a mile of dead-straight track where the gradient was gradual and over this stretch we reckoned to get up quite a good speed to carry us a good way up the incline. This was often frustrated by cattle being driven over the farm crossing, near the end of the straight, but with a good run we would get around the right hand curve and into the following left hand one before feeling the full weight of the load. The curve then became a little easier as we reached the old ground frame at Dulcote quarry. A ground frame is a miniature signal-box and in a single line section, entry is obtained by using a key on the end of the single line staff or token. We then had a steep climb and a sharp left bend with two wooden farm bridges over head. Just beyond this point on our right could be seen the vale of Avalon and Glastonbury Tor.

It was not unusual to come to a stand here and regain a good head of steam, but if not, we climbed on around the constant curves. Now the worse part of the climb came into sight; Three Arch Bridge. By this time steam and water would be very low and the fireman would be sanding the road to prevent the wheels slipping, and quite often we came to a stop and many times had to divide the train and send half forward. The rear section than had to be protected by detonators and the guards would do this at a distance of three-quarters-of-a-mile, rejoining the other part of the train when the engine returned for it. It was now only a short sharp climb to the summit coming to near level ground on the long curve just short of Shepton Mallet station. If we had parted the train, we could now join the two portions together again and proceed to Witham. The worst was over!

Rodeo in Easton* Cutting

When we travelled back to Wells with the 9:30 west depot freight, it was nearly always a tight squeeze to get through to Wells in front of the Yatton passenger. Delays were very important to us.

When we left Lodge Hill on the day in question, the signalman warned us that there was a pig on the line in the section, and ordered us to remove it if possible. The pig was soon found - it was walking in the middle of the track at the Westbury end of Easton Cutting. Dave the fireman got off the engine and tried to sneak past the old boar in order to drive it back past the engine.

There was a field gate just past it where the pig might have been turned off the line. Dave got past the pig and started to drive it back toward the engine, but then pig decided that it was scared of engine but not of Dave. It put its ugly head down, showed its tusks and charged. For a while Dave decided to bluff it out, and shouted abuse at pig. But pig kept coming and Dave decided to compromise. He ran up the bank still abusing pig in excellent verbal style.

Dave was firmly rooted to the cutting wall while pig stood watching him, and waiting for him to make the next move. So I thought I had better try moving pig past engine. Pig let me get past him toward Easton, then I ran at pig abusing him verbally as Dave had done. At first pig ran toward engine and then big black engine frightened big black ugly pig and he decided that I would be easier to move. He put his head down, showed his tusks and charged me. I didn't fancy getting those tusks in my leg and beat a strategic retreat up the steep cutting wall.

But Dave was now bawling at pig, so his attention was diverted between two of us and I suppose two of us must have equalled one big black engine. Anyway he ran past big black engine only to get on the track under the wagons. Dave came along looking for pig to drive it past the train. Pig looked him straight in the eye and from under the wagon charged. Dave stood swiftly aside and pig knocked him sideways, and bolted further up the cutting. The driver decided that the only thing to be done was to advance upon pig with cylinder-cocks open and hope that would induce pig to stand aside and let us pass. But he reckoned without pig's logical mind. As big black engine came up hissing steam out of the left hand cylinder, pig decided to go to the right hand side, only to find that big black engine hissed steam on that side too. In fact the only place that big black engine didn't hiss steam at him was in the middle of the track. So that is where he got.

Now, in front of a steam locomotive is a blind area where the driver cannot see. Low down, this blind area can be up to twenty-five feet in length, and pig was firmly ensconced in this blind area. Dave got off the engine and gradually hand-signalled his driver to move as long as pig kept moving. In this way in ten

* The Easton referred to is 3 miles from Wells on the Cheddar Road.

minutes we had gone a full hundred yards and in all that time the driver had not seen pig once. We were less than half way down the cutting. Dave was thoroughly fed up with pig by this time and plucked some big grass clumps from the wall of the cutting and threw them at, and hit pig with them.

The revolting pig revolted again. It charged again at Dave its ugly black head down and tusks showing. But Dave retreated only toward the brake van and jumped aboard, shouting to his driver to get moving. The driver opened the regulator and pig was left behind and the last we saw of him, he was still firmly in charge of the track.

We arrived at Wookey, gave up the single line staff and the signalman said, 'Where the hell have you been?' Dave said, 'Well, it's like this - on the way here we met a pig . . . .'

Stalactites

If you should go for a tour around Gough's or Cox's Cave at Cheddar, you will almost certainly be told that stalactites form at a rate of one inch per ten thousand years. Like other people I would have accepted this figure for the rest of my life but for something which I saw for myself. On the Cheddar valley branch line most of the buildings were built of a local stone. The station buildings (with the sole exception of Winscombe), the goods sheds (though not the signal-boxes), and most important to me, the bridges, were made of Draycott stone, from a quarry about midway between Wookey Hole and Cheddar, therefore of necessity the same type. But underneath the bridges were stalactites; some of them up to fifteen inches in length, and these bridges had been built less than one hundred years ago! Now I do not suggest that the conditions under the arch at Easton cutting and those in WookeyHole cave were in any way identical, but they had similarities which cannot be dismissed.

In both cases the stalactites were formed by the action of water seeping and leeching chemicals from the stone. But the difference between one inch per ten thousand years and fifteen inches per one hundred years is so great, that I just don't believe the former, nor will I; no matter how many argue the point. I say they must go back and think again and get it right this time.

45 class locomotive - the donkey of the branch lines - doing mainly passenger work. The engine had a particular fault - its small tanks needed constant refilling of water.

Runaways

Four sidings in the yard led from the inlet and were set by the shunters as required. The transfer from the upside to down was operated twice daily at midday and at midnight. The operation consisted of letting the transfer out by the wrong line through the inlet, engine first, then the engine propelled it through the main crossover to the down branch where it ran forward to the starting signal to be propelled into the down yard. On this night the transfer was waiting to depart when one of the shunters set the points for No. 1 siding by mistake instead of No. 5. His mate cut off a string of wagons and shunted them down to No. 1. When the wagons did not turn off to the right the shunter looked at the points and said to his mate, 'They are gone down No. 1. We had better get back or the transfer won't be able to go.'

His mate said, 'Oh dear, (or something), I've asked for the road for the transfer.' They ran up No. 1 and facing them was a green light in the ground signal but no wagons. The transfer was still standing for the driver had both heard and seen the wagons run into No. 1 and had tried to throw down a couple of brakes but had not been able to pin them down. The shunter told the signalman what had happened and the latter sent the bell signal 'train running away on wrong line' and asked the shunter how many wagons had been on the shunt. Neither of them knew exactly, but agreed it was about a dozen.

From the point where the wagons left the yard, to about a mile past the next signal-box was all down hill and then there was a slight rising gradient for about a quarter mile. The signal-box had no facing-points so that the wagons might be diverted. There were no catch points on the gradients so in a short while the signalman heard and saw the wagons approaching. They went by at a good forty miles-an-hour, but he was able to count them, fourteen!

Meantime the control had been alerted and had rung up Town South Box and asked the signalman there to try to get to Quarry Junction Box to turn the wagons into the Quarry branch if possible. Then he rang the facing junction next nearer to the wagons and told him to turn the wagons towards Quarry Junction. Having done this, the next thing was to find out how far the wagons had run and how far they would run. The man at the trailing junction box reported the passage of the fourteen wagons. The piece of rising gradient must have slowed the wagons down and everyone waited to see if they would stop.

The man at the facing junction box reported that he could hear the wagons approaching. At the same time the Town South signalman switched in Quarry Junction Box. The wagons could be heard by everyone now for all were listening to the telephone. They picked up speed again and passed the next box at about thirty-miles-an-hour. They sped on round the sharp bend but there was no noise of derailment.

There was an 'S' bend right by Quarry Junction Box and it would be touch and go if the wagons would negotiate the sharp double bend. The signalman held on to his levers and counted the wagons past; still fourteen. They reached the West Yard points and went on round the bend at a good mile a minute and they stayed on the track. Then they struck the uphill gradient. Nobody ever knew how far they went up the gradient but there was a good mile of it, and some three minutes later the man in Quarry Junction heard them returning. He had now set the points for the dead end. The leading wagon nearly reached the signal-box and then turned and ran back towards West Yard. In another five minutes they had come to rest. They had run over five miles. The yard inspector rode through the three sections on the shunting pilot, and searched the line in both directions. He let the wagons stay where they had come to rest, and ordered that they be thoroughly examined next day.

Fair are the Flowers in the Valley

The wild flowers in the Cheddar Valley are varied and numerous. There was a fair sample to be found along the old railway track between Yatton and Witham, but three flowers stick in my memory. There were wild daffodils in a couple of places, and the wild Iris (called flags) were to be found wherever there was water, but to me the valley flowers were the Evening Primrose, the Autumn Crocus and the Violets.

The Evening Primrose - I think its proper name is Onoethera - was a beautiful yellow flower growing to nearly five feet in height. No garden ever possessed a more graceful or beautiful flower. They grew in abundance in the carriage sidings at Tucker Street and alongside the little engine shed at Priory Road. There were also masses of them at the west end of Weston-Super-Mare station, but they were to me, the flowers of the valley. I knew where they grew at Wookey, at Lodge Hill and at Cheddar. If ever Somerset choses for itself a floral emblem I hope it will be the Evening Primrose.

The Autumn Crocus also has another name Meadow Saffron. It grew in its season in clumps where the grass was short and not too coarse. These clumps of slightly streaked purple flowers grew in many parts of the valley, but better upon the hills. There were patches of them near Congresbury and Winscombe, but the best were to be found high up between Shepton Mallet and Witham, and near Merehead Quarry grew a large clump of pure white ones - the only white ones I ever saw. I wonder if they still grow there.

The violets were almost everywhere but without any doubt the finest beds of violets, both blue and white, were on the down platform at Axbridge. Early in the year there were masses of flowers there, I hope they still survive. I wouldn't like to think that they disappeared with the railway.

Timber!

Jim was loading timber into a wagon for transit when the telephone bell rang. It was a special loud ringing bell attached to the goods shed wall, and it was necessary because the station was so small that often there was only one man on duty. Jim had to get out books to answer the telephone enquiry regarding demurrage, that is rental for a wagon standing under load. The station-master rang up. He was in charge of three small stations and demanded that Jim should wash out a cattle wagon which was standing in the cattle pens, and despatch it by the local freight. This he did, assisting the guard to pick up the empty cattle wagon. It took him to the end of his shift to complete and then he went home.

His mate was a younger man without Jim's dependability, so when later on the station-master rang up and asked if the wagon-load of timber was ready to go, the other man looked out of the window and saw the load apparently ready, and said, 'Yes, it's OK.' The station-master then ordered him to attach it to the afternoon freight and gave him instructions for labelling it. He made out the wagon labels, and did not examine the load, or he would have noticed that the load was protruding over the end of the wagon and needed to be roped. Jim had not had time to carry out this task.

The freight-train arrived, and the porter assisted the guard hitching up the load of timber. Here occurred the second fault. The guard did not notice the lack of rope. The load was very high at the start, the timber moved about as it started to settle down. Then the wagon hit a very bad joint and the top plank jumped on to the corner of the wagon. The end was now protruding over the side of the wagon as the train approached the station-master's own station. The bridge carrying the road over the track to join the station approach was cleared by about a foot, but then came the supporting pillars of the station canopy. They were made of stone.

The first, struck dead centre, collapsed with a tearing noise and load of dust. The signalman changing the single-line staff jumped well back from the canopy. The plank struck the second pillar which broke in half and the plank drove a hole in the other end of the wagon. The driver felt a snatch but didn't look back. The guard looked out and saw the canopy collapsing and did not see the reason for it as the plank was at that moment being driven through the end of the wagon. After the train had cleared the station he looked again but the plank was now not protruding.

He tried to attract the driver's attention but did not succeed. The train went speeding on, the guard had no clear view of the load of timber because the vehicles in-between were tall vans, so he had no idea what was happening to the loose plank. They approached the next little station. There was no signal-box here, but there was a level-crossing. Some freak of motion threw the plank over to the opposite side as it approached the porter's garden. Then it struck his pear tree and as it was torn out of the wagon, hundreds of nearly ripe pears fell from the tree. Never had fruit been so quickly harvested! But the hole in the end of the wagon was made larger by this wrench, and another plank went through it, and the train dragged it hard into the level-crossing. The crossing was partly rotten and was in fact due for renewal. Nevertheless the coupling snapped and the driver almost went through his window.

The permanent way gang heard the noise and came to see what aid they could give. They managed to draw out the part rotted crossing and there was nothing derailed. The wagon of timber was detached into the siding and the broken coupling did not affect the hook, therefore it was possible to reconnect. It was a rather lucky end to a potentially dangerous situation.

Answer the Phone Joe

The telephones with which the railway was equipped varied greatly from place to place, with their age, and with their purpose. A very common type consisted of a wooden cabinet about seven inches by five by three with a hook for the receiver and a separate ringing button, i.e. removal of the receiver from the dip did not ring the other bell. At a certain quite small yard, the shunters and guards had to wait a considerable time for Joe, the signalman, to answer, and since all movements were controlled by the signal-box, the delays mounted, and sometimes tempers flared.

One evening a guard decided that enough was enough. He dug the steel-shod end of his shunting pole into the soft gravel, and jammed the wooden end under the ringing button of the telephone. The bell began to ring continuously in the signal-box and Joe took his clip off to speak, but the guard had left the phone and walked away. With this type of phone the bell continued to ring and Joe could not stop it.

Soon Joe was at the window bawling out the guard to stop the bell ringing. The guard grinned to himself and ignored Joe, who was soon pleading with him to stop the bell. When the guard thought Joe had had enough to remember him by, he removed his shunting pole from the bell push, requested the necessary change of points, and when Joe called him a few choice names, he reminded the latter that he could do that at any time he chose, and Joe could do nothing about it. It brought about a considerable change in Joe's attitude to shunting.

Excursion to Weston-Super-Mare 1910s.

Stapleton Rd. Station about 1910. Note the change for Clifton and Avonmouth. Stapleton Rd. was a junction station. The Cardiff to Portsmouth service ran direct from there to Bath and did not go to Temple Meads. People therefore had to change from this service to get to Temple Meads.

Joe's Wages

Joe, the signalman, was telling his mate that he was about to draw his biggest wage packet ever. He had worked a long Sunday, his rest day (at overtime rate), and 12 hours each day for the week. Now Joe's signal-box was a quarter-mile from the station and usually a porter delivered Joe's wages and obtained a receipt, but on this day the staff had had a busy day and up to that point had not had time to do this. So Joe asked his mate Jim if he would please walk to the station and get his pay packet. Jim agreed and it was arranged by telephone that he would take Joe's wage packet and sign for it. This he did but as he was signing the book a small sack lying in the corner caught his eye, and his everlasting sense of mischief came to the fore. He would teach Joe about big pay packets!

He picked up the small sack, put Joe's wages in the bottom corner and tipped the contents of the office waste paper bin on top. This filled the little sack and he walked back to the box with it over his shoulder, and dumped it in front of Joe.

Joe said, 'What the h. . . . is this.'

'Your wages,' said Jim and 'twasn't half heavy!'

'Come off it,' said Joe, 'where's my pay packet!'

'In the sack,' said Jim. Joe squatted on the floor and started pulling out waste paper and throwing it down. Now there was an open fire in the signal-box and some of the paper got perilously close to it. Jim hurriedly pulled it away. This convinced Joe that his pay packet was indeed in the sack, but he was rapidly losing patience with the joke, and started to throw bits of paper everywhere. This alarmed Jim who was now really scared that he might burn or tear that precious pay packet. The joke was now very sour indeed, and Jim grabbed the sack from Joe, and retired to the corner of the box where he searched every bit of paper thoroughly and finally, much to his relief, came up with Joe's pay packet. Then he gathered up the waste paper, shoved it all in the sack, and a few minutes later when a freight train ran past the box, he dropped it into an empty wagon.

Jim swore that he would never under any circumstances ever play a practical joke with anyone's wages again, and he never did. Joe swore nothing, but he was never heard to discuss his wages with anyone after that.

The Strawberry Special

I arrived at Plymouth North Road with a special train and reported our arrival to the controller who said, 'Have a bite to eat, I have a return working for you.' Neither my driver or I fancied being landed with a freight to return with, for such a train might be by-passed a dozen times between there and Bristol. So we protested to control who replied that we would get home fast enough to suit anyone. Presently he sent us to the up platforms to take over a strawberry special which was just coming up from Millbay Docks. There was a fine Hall-Class engine and only about six bogied vans, capable of high speed and weighing less than 180 tons - a very light load indeed for a Hall-Class engine.

The strawberries had come from Brittany and were almost ripe and smelled very sweet. We climbed aboard and set off, making easy work of the load and fast time. I became aware of the pervading scent of the strawberries. I was well used to the smell of fruit, having served over nine years in the Cheddar Valley, but the valley strawberries were sent out a little short of ripe and therefore less scented. We topped Hemerdon Incline, and twisted our way in fine style round the Ivybridge bends and sailed down to Aller Junction.

By this time I had to open the van windows to get fresh air to counteract the sickly sweet scent of the fruit. I thought I might get stopped at Newton Abbot while the Paignton - Paddington express preceeded us, and I made up my mind I would get out and walk about, away from the smell of the fruit. Instead we had every signal in the off position and sped through Newton Abbot and on toward the sea at Teignmouth. Here I was hanging out of the window to get a smell of the sea and even the river Exe (beyond Dawlish Warren). Well, I would stretch my legs at Exeter because I was now feeling quite sick of the smell of the fruit. But every signal was clear at Exeter, and we went through as fast as the speed limits would allow. Well, I thought, maybe we would be put aside at Tiverton Junction or Sandford. No hope! Every signal was clear and we sailed on. Now I wanted to be sick, I put my head out of the window and tried to vomit but even that relief was denied to me. In spite of the open window, I had a headache and strangely my eyes hurt. We passed through Whitehall Tunnel into Somerset and the tunnel only concentrated the horrible sickly scent.

There were loops at Wellington where we might come to rest for a while. Forlorn hope! Every signal was off and we sailed through Taunton at high speed. I checked our times. From Plymouth to Whitehall must have been close to a record; but it seemed very long to me. I concentrated on trying to vomit but without success. In the confined van the strawberries were getting warm and consequently riper and more scented. Bridgwater passed - Highbridge and Uphill Junction were behind us. I hung my head from the window. I dare not withdraw into the van because I felt that I would pass out.

Fruit vans at Weymouth 1938. The vans are brand new.

Parson Street - Malago Vale - dirty old Bedminster, never have I been so glad to see them. At last Temple Meads - I was out of that van in three seconds. We had come from Plymouth absolutely non-stop in well under three hours but it had seemed so long to me. I haven't enjoyed strawberries since; indeed I never eat them if I can avoid it.

I worked strawberry specials quite often afterwards but I have never felt as sick again.

Cyril

When I first met Cyril he was a man in his middle fifties, a handsome, sparse man with a military style moustache, quiet and good-tempered but inclined to the practical joke. Two of us had worked freight trains to Westbury and a third Bristol guard was soon to arrive. Both of us reported to control by telephone and I was told to return home on the Salisbury mail. Control called Cyril and said, 'I want you for a certain freight train,' (mentioning its title). Cyril, thinking of the Bristol man soon to arrive in plenty of time to work the freight back, said over the phone to the controller, 'That's a pity, my wife is expecting. Control said, 'Hold on,' and called something across to his mate in the office. The telephone to his ear, Cyril waited. 'Did you say your wife was expecting,' asked control. 'Yes,' said Cyril. 'Then get off home on the Mail,' said control. 'Good luck!'

The following night when Cyril reported to control, the latter asked, 'How's the wife Cyril.' Cyril answered a bit surprised, 'Oh, she's all right.'

'And the baby?' asked control.

'What baby?' asked Cyril.

'I thought you said she was expecting,' said control. 'Oh yes,' said Cyril, 'she was expecting me home.'

I remember vividly Cyril's last day on the job. It was about a month before his 65th birthday. He came to the mess-room, sat down at our table, helped himself to a cup of tea, (I would have been offended if he hadn't) and announced, 'I have finished work, I am going home and won't do another stroke of railway work.'

'How can that be Cyril,' I asked. 'You aren't 65 yet.'

'No,' said Cyril, 'but the office discovered that I have a lot of leave due to me, so this is my last day. Do you know what I am going to do now? I am going home, I am going to get that old alarm clock out, wind it up, as if for half-past three in the morning, then I'll open the bedroom window, and throw the damned thing as far as my arm will carry it!'

Fred

Fred was a strong sturdy man of somewhat ruddy complexion, piercing grey eyes, with a twinkle always lurking somewhere around, and an aura of solid dependability.

Though he only worked on the small Wells branch line, he could handle a steam locomotive with almost unbelievable ease and accurancy. He should of course have been on the main line expresses where he would have been a king, but he preferred the little Somerset branch line. His knowledge of nature was vast and did not come from books, but from his own observations. From me he got first respect and then admiration. In those days I gave respect to extremely few men, and admiration to practically none.

I knew Fred to make only one mistake in his observations of nature, he used to tell me there were eagles in the valley. He told me even where they nested. I told him that the only eagles in Britain were in Scotland but he said, 'You will see.' I kept a careful watch on any large bird and Fred several times asked if I had seen them and I had to say no. Then one Sunday morning I was in charge of the engineers track laying train between Warnstow and Witham. The engine had been detached and with the workmen had gone ahead and I was alone with the van and a couple of wagons. The bird flew down, folded its great wing span and sat upon a fence-post not 25 yards from me. It was a beautiful peregrine falcon; a splendid specimen. I told Fred what I had seen but I found no pleasure in correcting him. I repeat that it was the only time.

He showed me so many things, for instance the fact that the falcons never appeared to menace the rabbits right under their nest sites; there seemed to be more rabbits at this spot than anywhere else in the valley. It was at this spot that Fred gave me an illustration of his marvellous observation. One day when travelling to Witham, Fred suddenly stopped (we had only the engine and van) and jumped off the engine and through the fence. As he did so I heard the unmistakable cry of a rabbit in its death throes. Fred ran across the field which was a full hundred yards; reached the fence next to the wood, bent down and picked up a still live rabbit and swiftly broke its neck. When I asked what had attacked the rabbit first, Fred said, 'A stoat, but he's lost his dinner today.' How he knew that at such a distance I shall never know.

He showed me where the squirrels congregated in the old quarry; grey ones of course, and the same quarry was the haunt of many owls. Another day we were climbing Doulting Cutting between Shepton Mallet and Cranmore when Fred stopped, jumped to a ledge in the cutting wall and shoved his left arm into a rabbit hole on the side of a jutting rock, and his right arm into another hole. He drew out a kicking rabbit with his right hand, and broke its neck with a blow from his left. 'That's dinner for tonight,' he said. He explained that the two holes were in fact joined together and he had been watching it for several days and had noted that a rabbit which went into the lower hole as we approached, was watching us from the upper one when we had passed.

I came to know the haunts of the badgers and foxes, and there were plenty of them in the valley, Fred knew them all. He was a fine man, a good mate, a great driver, and a really great self-taught naturalist.

Trunk Call

Ted was in charge of the 'Cornishman' one day when it topped the bank at Hemerdon and came to a stop. Now the up starting signal at Hermerdon had no track circuit, so although the train was in full view of the signalman, Ted was responsible for extra duties in the protection of his train, and he opened his door carefully and stepped out. On reaching the signal-box he saw that the signal in his rear had a collar on it and signed the train register, but the signalman was anxious to tell him that he had had a report that a red flag was flying from the train near the restaurant car.

'I'll search the train,' said Ted, 'do nothing more until I tell you.' He walked right round the twelve coaches of his train, explaining to the driver as he passed the engine and found nothing. Next he walked inside the train answering passengers' queries as best he could. A newspaper correspondent passenger asked him what was the matter, and this required some thought, for he knew that a garbled version of the facts would be frowned upon by management, and he answered that a call which he believed to be a hoax had been made to the signal man. As he reached the restaurant car, the chief steward drew him to one side into the kitchen. One of my lads came straight from bathing to the car,' he said. 'He wears red swimming trunks. I think he may have hung them to dry. They are here in this drawer.'

'I don't want to see them,' said Ted, 'but I hope they stay in that drawer.' 'They will, I can assure you,' said the chief. So Ted returned to the signal-box and wrote under his signature, 'Train searched nothing found.' He rejoined the train and the 'bobby' pulled off the 'board' and they got on with the job. Passing Teignmouth a young steward brought him a cup of coffee and started to apologise, but Ted said firmly, 'I don't want to know; see this?' and pointed to the note at the bottom of his journal. 'Red flag reported flying from train, searched inside and out, nothing found.' Such a method may seem to be a bit slack to the outsider, but it was the perfect way to make sure it never happened again.

Wrington Vale

I had orders to learn the route over the Wrington Vale branch. This ran from Congresbury to Blagdon; six-and-a-half miles, with three intermediate stations, and level crossings with and without gates. I arrived at Congresbury on the passenger train, hoping to catch the only train that used the branch, the freight train from Yatton. I had committed a technical sin in that I was not carrying my guards kit, merely my note book, my pencil and my sandwich bag. The signalman at Congresbury told me that the freight was already on the branch, so I said I would walk the six-and-a-half miles.

It was a cold but bright sunny day and a good walk was just what the doctor would order. Now on this branch there was a special instruction that the engineers had occupation each day except from half-an-hour before the freight train was due to leave Congresbury until half-an-hour after it had returned there. I walked on towards the first station - Wrington. This was where nearly all the work was done and frequently it was unnecessary for the train to proceed further, for the stations at Langford Burrington and Blagdon were very little used.

I came to Wrington to find that the train had already left, and to find also that the engineers had taken a rail out of the single track. I told the ganger that he had better put the rail back quickly, before the train could return, and he told me that the train had returned to Yatton and who did I think I was! and didn't I know the special instructions for the branch! I asked him how he thought the train could pass me without me seeing it or hearing it. He said he had heard it return to Yatton while they were having breakfast. I told him he had heard it depart toward Blagdon but he wouldn't listen.

I realised that I would have to get as far forward as possible in order to warn the Yatton crew on the train, and set off at a brisk pace. I regretted now that I had no kit, no detonators or red flag. I passed the saw-mill and went on around the very sharp bend. I was less than half-a-mile from Wrington when the train came around the bend towards me. I stood in the track until the last moment both arms upraised, then I had to jump. I shouted at the fireman who put his head out of the little engine. I pointed toward Wrington and shouted 'Rail out.' I shouted again as the guard came to the door of his van, and in about ten seconds it was gone. I waited for the sound of the crash, but none came. I pondered whether I should walk back the half-mile to Wrington but decided that whatever had happened I would be of no help, and I was now hopeful that somehow trouble had been avoided.

I went on and completed my survey of the branch and ate my sandwiches on a beautiful sunny day where everything was at peace around me. I walked part way back to where I could catch a bus to Axbridge and returned from there by train and booked off.

It was a very long time afterwards before I elicited the truth from one of the Yatton men. Apparently the engineering gang considered what I had said and overruled their ganger and the moment my back was turned on them, started to restore the rail and had just succeeded when the train arrived. The train crew were left wondering what, 'that idiot up round the corner' - meaning me - was shouting about.

The Stop Board

Not so long ago there were few or no vacuum or air brakes in freight trains. So the practice in descending inclines was as follows. The driver stopped his engine at a board which was marked "stop and apply brakes" or sometimes just S.B. The guard then left his van, taking with him a stout brake stick which was square in section at one end and ended at a smooth handle and was about 3½ feet long. Now the driver pulled his train slowly on to the incline and the guard would pin down hand brakes on the wagons, having the brake stick to obtain sufficient leverage. When the driver felt he had sufficient brake power he would blow the whistle, and the guard would rejoin his van. Usually one brake for six wagons was about correct.

I had one driver whose call for brakes I considered excessive and unnecessary, and one day this driver stopped at the top of an incline with only four wagons on the train, and wanted me to apply hand brakes. So I left the van feeling pretty disgruntled, and his fireman was grinning at me knowing full well what I was thinking. In order to make him wait till I felt like it, I decided to relieve my bladder. There was an ant-hill by the stop board fully twenty inches high, and I let my urine flow over it - then I jumped well away from it - but not as far or as fast as the rabbit which had been squatting unseen on the other side.

Cranmore

Cranmore station is high and windy. I believe the local people are made with a little steel in them; for in winter it is a wild and bitter place to be. The snow there starts earlier and lasts longer than anywhere else in Somerset. It had, in the fifties, a nickname (which I will later tell you) by which it was known for a radius of forty miles around indicating the severity of its winters. The new station master arrived late one summer, he was enchanted by the countryside and enthused about it; he was warned by many of us not to overenthuse, but to wait the arrival of winter, but he just wouldn't believe us. He obviously thought we were exaggerating everything; and maybe we were just a little.

One day in 1949, just after his arrival I picked up some wagon sheets at Witham; they were very heavy and I needed the assistance of my fireman to lift them into the van. Similarly when I arrived at Cranmore I needed assistance to offload them and I picked on the new station master to do so. As we worked we talked - he told me straightly that he thought we were all pulling his leg about the winter conditions. 'Well mister,' said I, 'look at those wagon sheets - they arrived without any misunderstanding.' He looked at the sheets - there was no label to indicate where they were to go, instead scrawled in chalk was the legend . . . . Sunny Siberia.

Cellophane

Travelling at night on fast passenger trains, one of the difficulties of the guard is to know exactly where he is. The driver is not confused as is the guard. He sees the road ahead as a kind of film. It is continuous to him. Indeed he is looking ahead for the next clue all the time. The guard has to pick out selected points and check the times between them for he is the official timekeeper of the train but he had many aids in the sounds of the journey. The crossing at Highbridge had a most distinct sound due to the fact that it was one massive casting whereas most crossings are made up of rails and sleepers.

The track between Hewish crossing and Yatton always sounded hollow; why I do not know. With the standardisation of tracks, many of these sounds have disappeared. But there was one place which could be identified - by smell at any time. The cellophane works on the Bristol side of Bridgewater. I find it impossible to describe the smell. It was quite different from any other. Oh - with one exception - that was at a factory where they made artificial pearls; at Manacor in Majorca.

Tales from the 50s and 60s

Bankers

On the railway a bank was not so much a place of safe deposit, neither was it always the shores of a river. It usually meant a steep incline. A banker was not the custodian of your money, or a "dead certainty", but an assistant engine.

In the days of steam locomotives there were many inclines where it was necessary to keep bank engines constantly. Many of these inclines had special instructions, and there were various ways of using the assistant engine. In some places such as Bromsgrove, for the "Lickey" incline, the only locomotives kept were for assistance and the shed had no other use; so as engines got larger, and the demand for assistance less, the shed could be abolished, and the bank engines came from Birmingham. Old time guards have told me of having three or four bankers up the "Lickey", but I never had more than one.

Between Pilning and Severn Tunnel Junction all assistance was on the front. The bank engines were nearly all 2-6-2 tanks, though a few 0-6-2 tanks were in use. They were all powerful class D engines. At the east end of the Severn Tunnel there were four separate places at which the banker could be attached, and as there could be as many as six freight trains waiting at the various points, the only indication the trainman had that he was next to go, was the arrival of the banker.

Sometimes a banker was attached though no request had been made for one. This was usually because the engines had all got to one end, and a balance had to be kept. The engines came from the Severn Tunnel Junction shed, and the tunnel inspectors usually managed to arrange it so that a driver was working towards home shortly before his duty time was up. There were two points of attachment at the west end, but because of the nature of the traffic (coal, iron castings, rolled steel etc) almost every up train required a banker.

If these trains were heavy enough, and many of them were, they had to be assisted through to Patchway, and to do this, the banker was removed from the front at Pilning and brought to the rear, where it assisted unattached to Patchway. The up and down tunnels in this section are separate, with a single line in each, and this is the section many of us dreaded. The up tunnel with only a single line, was very slow to clear of smoke, and the guard and banker crew were often almost choked here. Naturally the banker crew kept up the maximum possible speed to get out of the tunnel as rapidly as possible. However, the smoke created another hazard; it was a very dirty tunnel, and the rails were shiny with much use and greasy from the smoke. The locomotives frequently slipped. If the leading engine slipped, the train (and the banker) got a severe bump from the rear. If the banker slipped, the train would first get a snatch then as the banker caught up, a real good bump. Since it was virtually impossible for drivers to detect the slip, especially in the smoke and gloom of Patchway "up", it was often a very rough ride indeed.

The two parallel (well almost) banks of Stapleton Road to Filton Incline, and Engine Shed junction to Fishponds, were both worked with the banker at the rear unattached. At Engine Shed (or Lawrence Hill junction) the banker was let out behind the train, and overtook it on the move, but at Stapleton Road, the train was stopped and restarted.

From Avonmouth to Filton West junction, the banker was attached at the rear because the gradients were both rising and falling. Trains were booked to stop at Filton West to detach the banker, but the common practice was for the guard to detach the banker on the run down the aerodrome straight, by leaning over the end of the van, and lifting the engine coupling off his hook with the shunting pole. He then hand-signalled both drivers that he had uncoupled, and provided the signals were off, the train did not stop. The rules were bent, but the men were skilled, and no trouble ever came of this practice.

On the Cheddar valley line there were three steep banks, Wells-Shepton Mallet, Witham-Cranmore and Axbridge-Winscombe, but no assistance was ever provided for any of them, and only single engine loads could be carried. The Yeovil Pen Mill to Evershot bank was worked as a combination of two methods. Bankers were attached from Yeovil to Yetminster, and could run un-attached from there to Evershot. So sometimes the guard detached the banker at Yetminster, but more often, it was sent in advance to Yetminster. Then the train did not stop there, and the banker was released from the siding and over-took the train on the run. This manoeuvre had to be carried out with great care by the banker driver but I never heard of anyone being hurt while carrying it out.

Other West of England banks where banking had to be performed on a reg-ular basis were Plympton (to Hemerdon), Castle Cary (to Brewham), Aller Junction (to Dainton), Holt Junction (to Devizes) and Wellington (to Whiteball Tunnel). As more and more powerful diesel engines came into use the bankers were phased out and the practice has now disappeared.

Whippit

We had a goods guard at Temple Meads who was probably the greatest practical joker the station had ever seen. He had a nickname taken from a radio series of the period "Whippit Quick" and he was known as Whippit to many who didn't even know his proper name.

It was in 1956 when the railways had not yet recovered the timing habits of pre-war years; a time when men might book on, on Tuesday, just in time to work Monday's train; a time when consequently many men spent a great deal of time "in the cabin*". Therefore it was necessary if you made a can of tea, to retain possession of the can until you had taken your own cupfull, otherwise it would be emptied for you. It was the commonly accepted practice to help yourself to anyone's tea once they had filled their cup.

There was nearly always one, and sometimes two cardschools going, and Whippit was a frequent member of a school. He was seated one afternoon playing cards and studiously ignoring everything else (which meant that in reality he was seeing everything), when George made his tea in his big blue can. George then made the error of leaving the can while he washed up a cup. Whippit stood up casually, opened No. 78 locker (the keys were hanging in the lock) put George's can in the locker, and sat down and concentrated on the game in hand. It was done so casually and yet so quickly, that even his fellow players did not realise what he had done.

He now concentrated on the game and waited for the outcry when George returned. He so studiously avoided looking at the locker, that he genuinely did not see the owner of No. 78 turn the keys in the lock, slip them into his pocket and go on home. George returned and looking everywhere for his can, was soon fuming. Whippit presently looked up and said, 'You put your can in the locker George I'm sure you did!' George opened his locker which was No. 75 and with forceful expletives asked, 'Where the . . . . is it then?' Whippit's jaw dropped. 'No George, yours is No. 78,' he said. 'That's Jack's locker,' said George, 'and he's gone home!'

'I'm sure you used No. 78,' said Whippit. He put his nose to the keyhole, 'Yes I can smell fresh tea,' he said, and standing back, 'look there's steam coming out of the keyhole; you've made a mistake George, you put your can in Jack's locker. Never mind I'll make tea now and you can have the first cup.'

* Locker and messroom.

An Easter Weekend

Ted worked the Manchester from Bristol to Taunton on the Thursday at tea-time. In the country approaching Bridgwater the brakes went on. An examination of the vacuum gauge showed that the driver was endeavouring to regain control of the brake and not succeeding. This could mean only one thing, the communication chain had been pulled.

Ted looked out as the fireman got down from the engine, and they started to walk towards each other. Ted found the indicator first. Railwaymen call it a 'butterfly'. It shows which coach the chain has been pulled in and has to be put back from outside the coach. In this case Ted climbed into the coach and noted where the chain was hanging loose, then turned the butterfly and told the fireman to proceed to Bridgwater which was a booked stop for the Manchester. The coach was open-centred and he found a lady collapsed over a table. Fortunately there was an older lady who had taken over very successfully. She belonged to the WVS and told Ted that the younger lady had had an epileptic fit but it was obvious that the worse was now over. Ted searched the younger lady's handbag while the other watched. In this way without bothering the patient he found her name and address in Birmingham, and her ticket which gave her destination as Minehead.

Having obtained the WVS lady's name and address, Ted turned to the young man who had pulled the communication chain. He appeared to think he had been quite clever, until Ted asked him if he realised that he had actually prevented the train from reaching a town, an ambulance and a doctor. He took his name and address and the foolish young man said, 'What did you expect me to do.' Ted said, 'Any time this sort of thing occurs you fetch the guard, and don't stop the train.'

They drew into Bridgwater, Ted left the staff to deal with his van, while he got hold of the best first-aid man in the place. He wanted the examiner's opinion about the advisability of the patient travelling further. Both the examiner and the WVS lady thought that she might be left to continue her journey. They arrived at Taunton and the WVS lady took her patient into the refreshment rooms. Ted fetched the inspector, gave him the particulars, and asked if the Minehead train would have corridor coaches. The inspector asked why and Ted told him that he thought the patient must be in contact with the guard at all times. She could do herself a lot of harm if she had another fit in a non-corridor compartment. Remember that this took place nearly twenty years ago and the drugs for controlling epilepsy were not in use. Ted left the whole thing in the hands of the inspector and went to the up side for his return working. As the up train was running in he heard a public announcement asking any doctor to go to the down side refreshment rooms. It was three weeks before he worked into Taunton with the same inspector on duty, so that he could ask what had happened.

It appeared that the lady had had another fit in the refreshment rooms and a doctor had been found by the public address system. He would not guarantee the lady's safey on the Minehead train which was non-corridor stock. In any case the guard refused to take her. An ambulance had been called, and she had spent the Easter weekend in hospital and had been taken back to Birmingham on the Tuesday with a medical escort.

In these days of good drugs for epilepsy control, this would never happen. Indeed epileptics today may travel in safety almost anywhere.

The Atomic Flask

I was at Worcester Shrub Hill, waiting to attach and detach with the afternoon Droitwich to Stoke Gifford, when the word came through of an accident on the main line between Abbotswood Junction and Cheltenham. A partly vacuum fitted freight for Exeter was in front of us also working, when the examiner 'red-carded' the vehicle conveying the atomic flask. The examiners red card was worded 'not to go' and it meant exactly what it said, until the repairs listed upon it had been carried out.

The atomic flask was on a special vehicle and it carried atomic waste between the generating station and the dumping site. The flask in question was to go to Hinkley Point power station. So the yard inspector got in touch with the generating board who urged him to make the stoppage of the flask as short as possible. It was detached on to a nearby siding and the repairers sent for.

In the meantime, the crew of the Exeter freight were asked about route knowledge. As all of them knew the route via Honeybourne, the train was sent forward by the diverted route. We pulled forward to do our stint and while I was rewriting my train tally, I was also asked if I could take the diversionary route, and I had to refuse for the lack of route knowledge. Then to my surprise the examiner came back and said the flask had been repaired and was ready to go! The job had only taken an hour. We now attached the flask and prepared to wait for clearance of the main line.

A second miracle! The main line was now clear and we could proceed. We had a good run and immediate attention at Gloucester South Yard, and we pulled into Stoke Gifford down loop still with daylight to spare. The part vacuum freight, from which the flask had first been detached, arrived an hour later at Stoke Gifford where it was specially side-tracked to attach the flask that it had detached at Worcester.

The Swansea Pullman

In the sixties, Ted Myers was a goods guard at Temple Meads. He was a senior hand and was doing a spare turn one morning when he was called to the telephone. Control told him to travel as passenger to Severn Tunnel Junction to bring back an Exeter freight. Ted asked if the train could be prepared for him, to save time, and control agreed to do so. So when he arrived at Severn Tunnel Junction, he found the train ready to go at the middle signal-box. He therefore did not examine the train at all, but told the driver the load and got on board the van.

As the train went over the rise at the end of the platforms, Ted applied the brakes gradually but nothing happened. The train ran into the running loop with the engine doing all the braking. The passenger train ran past them and barely stopping, Ted's freight ran on out of the bottom end of the loop and headed for the Severn Tunnel itself.

Now I hope my reader will excuse me if at this point I explain the vital importance of a good brake. If a freight train with loose couplings is suddenly jerked forward then almost certainly a coupling somewhere on the train will break. After all, the total weight of such a freight train is in the region of a thousand tons. Now at the bottom of the Severn Tunnel such a snatch will undoubtedly take place unless the train is already stretched tight by the application of the rear brakes. When the whole of the train is on the upward slope the brake can be released.

Ted tried frantically to get some brake power on as the Severn Tunnel enclosed them, and the brake-wheel screwed up tight without any reasonable effect. His hand-lamp was alight, and after about a quarter mile he suddenly saw by its lights that the brake-wheel had worked loose.

Ted reapplied the brake, and suprisingly now found that the brake really pulled hard. He gradually applied more pressure and he could feel the train being stretched out under the influence of the van brake. Therefore, they passed the bottom well stretched out, and without any snatch at all. Ted was very relieved but extremely puzzled at the behaviour of the brake.

They left the tunnel and headed into the running loop leading to Pilning. Ted tried to attract the attention of the Severn Tunnel East signalman but was unable to do so. As soon as the train came to a stand, Ted applied the brake which held very well, and jumped out onto the ground to examine his van.

What he saw really frightened him. All the rear brake gear was torn away. This included four of the sixteen brake blocks leaving the other twelve firmly on the wheels.

The hanging bars and a large stretcher bar, about fifteen hundredweight of steel, was missing and Ted's experience told him that it must have been torn off at the point when he reapplied the brake. He ran ahead to the telephone at the signal and frantically rang the phone bell, signalling with his hands to the signalman whom he could just see in the box. The signalman answered the phone.

Ted said, 'Stop The Tunnel, send 'obstruction danger'.' The man said, 'What's the matter?' Ted said, 'Stop The Tunnel first and then come back to the phone - I'm not going anywhere.'

He heard the block-bells start ringing and heard the acknowledgement of the 'obstruction danger' signal and was very relieved. 'Now', said the bobby, 'What is it all about.' (on the railway all signalmen are bobbies). Ted explained the situation saying that there was the better part of a ton of brakework on the track in the tunnel. He went back to the van. A few minutes later the inspection van with its brilliant lighting drew up opposite him and the inspector called over to him, 'Where do you think the brakework is Ted?'

'About a quarter of a mile in, on the Welsh side,' said Ted. He was still there when the inspection van reappeared with the gear slung aboard.

The inspector put a temporary speed limit on the up line and traffic started to move again. The first train to emerge from the tunnel was the Swansea Pullman. The following week Ted Myers was given a passenger guard's job. One of his turns involved travelling to Swansea by the first train. He reached this turn seven weeks later and while eating his meal in Swansea guards' room, a younger Swansea guard came in and said to one of his mates, 'The last time I did this job some fool of a goods guard reported a bump in the Seven Tunnel and held us up for an hour!'

Ted looked at him, opened his log book and asked what date that might be. It was of course the day when Ted saved the Pullman from an almost certain wreckage. So he owned up and the young Swansea man left in an embarrassed hurry.

St Philips Marsh locomotive shed, Bristol. The modern Fruit and Vegetable Market now stands on this site.

Catch Points

We must start this tale with an explanation of what a catch point is. It is a point in the track where a train going in the correct direction closes against the springs and can pass with safety. If a train should attempt to pass in the wrong direction, i.e. a runaway broken section, it will become derailed through the open point. These catch points are placed on steep gradients so as to derail a breakaway before it can do much damage, or run across junction points. On long gradients it is sometimes necessary to have two or even three catch points.

One Sunday, on such a gradient, engineering work was proceeding on the down line, while the up line was in use as a single line. In order to do this, it is necessary to clamp the catch points in the closed position and to padlock them and to appoint a ground signalman to hand signal trains over the catch points, indicating that they are safely closed and padlocked. On this particular Sunday it had been a long and arduous days work, starting at five in the morning and being completed twelve hours later; this is the only excuse that can be offered for what followed.

A train was due at the top of the incline, to travel down it, and the engineer in charge told the signalman on the telephone to hold it until he arrived with the engineers' special on the line which had been closed i.e. the down line. He then intended to sign the certificate handing over the down line to operation, but he didn't say so. He intended that the next train at the top of the incline should then travel on the correct, newly opened down line.

So he started *up* the down line and picked up the hand-signalmen on the way and unlocked and released the three catch points on the up line, which he should not have done, until he had first handed over the certificate. They had just got started, after picking up the last hand signalman, when they saw to their horror a passenger train approaching in the down direction on the up road, and heading for the now open catch points.

The driver blew his whistle, the fireman, the guard and a couple of engineers jumped off the train showing red lights and red flags (it was just dusk). The driver of the passenger train saw them just too late - he braked and his locomotive had the bogie derailed, which was in the circumstances very fortunate, for much worse damage might have been done. The only thing suffered by any passenger was inconvenience.

The Gas Works Excursion

Jack was a real countryman, hard working, transparently honest, knew his job, helpful to others, but a trifle naive; he was a perfect subject for one of Whippit's jokes. Duties have often to be allocated on the basis of route knowledge. For instance for a train to Weston-Super-Mare almost any guard would know the route and would be sent to cover it. Other routes perhaps only a few guards would know.

When Whippit called from an outside phone, pretending to be the controller, he knew well who was in the cabin and the extent of their route knowledge. He called this day and asked if there was anybody who knew the route to Nottingham, knowing that the only person who would claim this was Jack.

'Put him on,' said Whippit. 'That you Jack? Well this is the position. There is an excursion train in Stapleton Road Gas Works, on the Midland side. The passengers are being brought to the train in coaches. There are steps provided to embark them. The point is, the train must run non-stop to Nottingham. Think you can manage that Jack?'

'Oh yes,' said Jack.

'Very well then,' said Whippit. 'Off you go!'

Jack packed his traps* and was on his way out when Whippit strolled in. 'Where are you going Jack,' he asked. Jack told him. 'Go on,' said Whippit, 'somebody is pulling your leg.'

'No they are not,' said Jack. 'I've had my orders.'

'Halt a minute,' said Whippit. 'I'll ring the controller and see what he says, I'm sure there's a mistake here somewhere.' But Jack wouldn't wait and marched off.

The rest of us taunted Whippit, 'You have done it this time. He'll murder you when he gets up to the gas works.' So Whippit went after Jack and continued to tell him that the controller knew nothing about any such excursion and was sure that someone was pulling his leg. Jack said that he could recognise the controller's voice and he wasn't going to listen to a notorious leg-puller like Whippit.

They walked the length of Temple Meads platform still arguing. On they went, past the East Box and around the corner to Engine Shed Junction where Whippit persuaded Jack to wait while the signalman phoned the control to substantiate what he had been saying.

I don't know what passed between the signalman and the controller but since both knew Whippit's reputation well, I imagine it was very different from what the signalman told Jack. He said, 'Control says you are to return to the cabin. They have found a Nottingham guard to do the job.'

The joke I know went round the control office for some time that Whippit had been beaten by his own cleverness. I just wonder at what point Jack rumbled Whippit and decided that two could play games like that.

* Kit, including handlamp.

Post Second War standard steam engines. They did not have a very long life because of fast en-

There and Back

Alan was a goods guard, a very efficient, knowledgable, and (normally) alert man in his 50s at the time of this incident. But he had been moonlighting (i.e. doing another job in off-duty hours). I first heard the term at about this time, so perhaps it was invented for Alan. One night he worked a freight train from Bristol to Worcester Shrub Hill, contacted the controller on the phone, and was told to go home on the "mail". This was just after two in the morning. As soon as the "mail" arrived, Alan found himself a corner seat in an empty compartment and went to sleep. He slept so soundly it was almost unbelievable. He saw and heard nothing of Cheltenham or Gloucester, and the train completed its run at Bristol Temple Meads. Until now there was nothing remarkable about it, but the rest will take some swallowing, nevertheless it is true.

A porter at Temple Meads saw Alan asleep, opened the door, shouted, 'Come on Alan - Temple Meads,' and walked away. Alan only felt the cold when the door was opened, roused himself and shut the door again, without recognising where he was, and went to sleep again. The porter saw what he had done, and having done his part, shrugged his shoulders and did no more about it. The locomotive arrived from Barrow Road and soon the coaches were being hauled back to Lawrence Hill Junction and dropped into the Midland carriage sidings. Here they were thoroughly cleaned; and still Alan slept, while the windows were washed, and even while a man swept the floor around his feet. This particular man owed Alan a grudge, so he was careful not to wake him. His mates in the cleaning gang thought it was a great joke and made no effort to wake him. The cleaning finished, the night staff went home and forgot about him.

At seven o'clock a locomotive backed on to the coaches and was coupled up. They were then drawn up to the main line and backed into the old station on No. 12 platform, and were ready to return North. At 7:25 the train pulled out with Alan still asleep in his corner. All the night staff had gone home, so there was nobody to know that anything unusual was happening. The fact that it had been broad daylight for some time had no effect upon Alan who slumbered on.

The train stopped at Gloucester and Alan stirred for the first time, looked out and recognised Gloucester Eastgate station and made a mental note that he could get another forty minutes sleep before he reached Bristol, and dropped off again. The train stopped again. Alan thought,'Must be near Charfield by now,' when someone shouted, 'Cheltenham, Cheltenham?' how could that be? Alan grabbed his lamp and kit and opened the door. As he got out the train started to move and in the opposite direction to the way Alan expected. He fell sprawling on the platform, and a porter chased after the door and closed it. Alan now realised that he was on the up platform and not the down. He looked at his watch. It said 8:25 which was ridiculous (at least it was according to Alan). Unfortunately the station clocks agreed with his watch. The foreman spoke to Alan but he thought it wiser to ignore the man until he had got the situation sorted out. He walked over the bridge still working out the facts. A down train ran in and Alan got on it. He now realised how long he had slept. He was wide awake now.

He couldn't face going to the goods guards' cabin, in case someone knew all about it, and they probably would by now. So on arrival at Bristol he hid his kit in a place known only to him, and sneaked out via the goods depot. On arrival home his wife was getting rather anxious and was about to call up the Guards Inspector. Alan said, 'If anybody asks, I've been home since just after four this morning.' He was still telling her a part of what had happened when the telephone rang. It was the inspector's time-keeper. 'Is Alan at home?' he asked. 'Yes,' said his wife, 'he got in just after four this morning.'

'Then please tell him,' said the time-keeper, 'to book off in the proper manner in future. We thought something had happened to him.'

Pigeons

Sid Brown was sent out to work a pigeon special from Hereford to Bristol. 'Are you ready?' asked the inspector. 'If so I'll get the road.'

(This means I will inform the signalman that you are ready to leave).

'Not yet,' said Sid. 'I haven't seen the convoyer yet.' The convoyer was a man employed by the pigeon federations to look after the birds during their journey. Sid found the convoyer who said he needed water for the birds. They fetched out three milk churns of ten gallons capacity each and put the first under the tap.

Before the churn was half-full, the inspector was out blowing his whistle and demanding their departure. Sid said, 'I told you not to get the road because we are not ready, we shall be here until we have filled the drums.'

The inspector said he needed the platform for a passenger train, but Sid said, 'You have another track, use it!' The argument got quite heated but the convoyer settled it by saying, 'If you don't shut up I will report this matter to the R.S.P.C.A. I don't think the railway management will relish a prosecution.'

Bristol Traversing Yard Crane at St Philips Marsh. Probably one of the strongest cranes in the area. In existence till the 1970s.

Locking Road

Developments at Locking Road Station at Weston-Super-Mare provide a good comment on what has happened to British Rail. It is now a coach and car park, but in the forties and fifties it was a busy excursion terminal station. It had four platforms, and one of them had a ground frame at the town end, so that the engine could be released. It could then be used to pull the next train away and shunt its coaches into a siding. Then there would be two engines available - and so on.

The main use of Locking Road Station was at bank holidays for excursion trains. An average holiday would mean between 20 and 25 excursions. Of course the staff at Weston-Super-Mare could not be left to cope with this sort of traffic, though many of them would serve their shift at the general station, and then go to Locking Road for overtime. Staff from out-stations who would otherwise have been off-duty for the day, were sent to Locking Road. These men were granted a day off in lieu of the bank holiday later on in the year and usually they preferred this arrangement. These together with all the relief who could be spared made up the manning level for a long hard day.

If it was a hot day (as all the customers hoped) then every window on every train would be open and have to be closed, for it might well rain hard before the train returned, and wet seats would not induce passengers to travel by train. Every compartment had to be swept out, and the mounds of rubbish cleared away. The examination of the coaches inside and out, was very important. Frequently broken windows were found and the glass had to be cleared. Many of the coaches could not be accommodated at Weston and had to be returned to Yatton or Bristol, and then brought back again in good time for the return working. The fact that none of this is required today, reveals the changes that have come to our habits. Is it any improvement?

A Dangerous Practice

I came into the yard one day just as the gang who had been cleaning up set fire to some straw. I ran for a big wooden rake which used to stand in the corner of the locker room, dashed out with it and started to drag the burning straw away from the petrol depot. The man looked at me with suprise. 'It's safe enough,' said one. 'The tanks are empty they won't catch fire.'

I agreed, but said they might explode. At this they all laughed. I said to the sub ganger, 'You run a motorbike don't you? Now, what does it burn?'

'Petrol,' said he.

'If that is so why do you need a carborator.'

Said one platelayer, 'It doesn't burn petrol, it explodes vapour.'

'Right,' said I, 'so remember that in future empty tanks can be more dangerous than full ones.'

The 'Owl'

The engineering train arrived and the signalman told the driver to go ahead, to clear the siding points in order to be side-tracked from the path of the Paddington to Penzance passenger and mail, nicknamed the 'Owl'. The signalman reversed the points and the guard called the driver back by hand-signalling with his hand-lamp. Next to the engine was a long bogied vehicle which was over 40 feet in length between the bogies. Engineers were walking about just below the signal-box. One of them called out to his mate over some measurement. 'All right now.' The signalman thought it was the driver telling him that the train was inside the siding, and put the points back into normal position. He was able to do this as the points, at that moment, lay between the two bogies of the bolster wagon. However, the fireman heard the points move and shouted to the driver to stop. He then shouted to the signalman that the train was still fouling the main line.

Meanwhile the 'Owl' which had been standing at the home signal, started to move as the signalman pulled the signal off. The signalman immediately put the signal back to danger, but the driver of the 'Owl' did not see it and opened the throttle. The signalman meantime reversed the points and shouted to the driver of the engineering train to get back into the siding. The fireman jumped from the engine with his hand-lamp showing red toward the 'Owl'. The guard heard the shouts and although he did not know what was wrong, he also jumped off the van and showed the 'Owl' a red light.

What really saved the situation was the weight of the 'Owl' which prevented any great acceleration, and gave a little time to these men working desperately to avoid the imminent collision. The 'Owl' passed the guard without seeing his red light, and the noise of the great steam engine drowned his frantic shouting. The driver of the engineering train saw that he was now inside the points and blew three blasts on the whistle which was the correct signal to the signalman. The signalman slammed the points back to normal. The driver in the siding blew a long-long blast on his brake whistle; the driver of the 'Owl' heard it and saw the fireman's red light and braked hard.

He came to a stand on the points. After a few hurried words with the engineer who examined the points under the wheels of the "Castle", the 'Owl' pulled away again. As its tail light disappeared in the night, everyone relaxed and sighs of relief were heard all round. It had been so very close to disaster.

Abergavenny Junction

In the fifties, the trains from the north-west i.e. Liverpool, Manchester and Glasgow ran via Shrewsbury, Hereford, Maindee Junction (near Newport) and the Severn Tunnel into Bristol and thence to Devon and Cornwall. On Friday nights - early Saturday mornings in the summer a large number of extra trains were run to get holiday makers to their destinations. This has now largely been replaced by car traffic on the motorways, and all the north to west trains run via Birmingham and Gloucester. But at the time I write of, a dozen crews would ride to Shrewsbury each Friday night to work the extra trains through the night.

One early Saturday morning I was working a Liverpool to Paignton extra, and we were bowling along satisfactorily through the night when an old man wandered into my van and started to talk. He wasn't able to sleep and wanted something to break the monotony. I understood and he was welcome anyway; it was a long boring trip from Shrewsbury to Bristol. I had an old Midland type van right at the end of the train. These had two window type seats, but they were not very stable, in fact they sometimes swayed dramatically, so I asked the old gentleman to sit down in the unused seat. He declined, saying he wanted to stretch his legs. I warned him about the swaying propensity of that type of van but he stayed on his feet.

I felt the speed start to increase sharply and realised that we were approaching Abergavenny Junction. I said, 'Please sit down sir.' He would not. I heard the engine hit the points. I shouted, 'Grab the grille and hold tight.' My tone of voice made him obey this time. Then the van jerked violently three times and he almost lost his grasp of the grille. He turned very white. I said, 'It's all right now sir.' He came and sat down. He said, 'Is it often like that,' and I assured him that there were very few places quite as bad as Abergavenny Junction.

Barbering

Wally was the part-time barber in the locker room. If it became obvious that a man was going to be some time waiting for a train he would ask Wally for a haircut and would get one. However, Wally was frequently on spare duties which meant he could be called to cover any emergency which arose. Such men were picked for their knowledge of as many routes as possible, and Wally was an old hand with wide route knowledge.

One morning just before nine, Wally started to give one of his mates a haircut. Whippit noted this and walked out and into a neighbouring office and called the locker room on the telephone. To the guard answering the phone he said, 'Inspector's office - tell Wally to get his gear and come on up and work the nine o'clock London.' Whippit then strolled back into the cabin to note the panic he had caused. The nine o'clock London I should explain, was the great prestige train of the day at that time and Wally was scambling to get his barber's kit put away, and his guards kit out at one and the same time. The customer in the chair was asking what Wally intended to do with him, and Whippit suggested that he should go with Wally on the nine o'clock as far as Bath which was the only stop, and Wally could then cut his hair between Bristol and Bath.

Wally was the type of barber who started at one ear and worked gradually round to the other. He had got about half way round on this occasion. There was only one man in the locker room who didn't see the funny side of it and that was Wally's customer.

Whippit strolled out again and went to the office phone. After about three minutes of absolute chaos, and just as Wally was about to leave, the phone rang again. The man who answered it was told, 'Tell Wally the booked man has now turned up for the nine o'clock and he is not now required.'

———————

Tales from the 1970s

Skittled

The junction box was very, very long. Its frame held over one hundred levers but even so there was a lot of room at either end. It was worked by one signalman and a booking boy on each turn, and so at two o'clock each afternoon there were, for a short time, four people in the box, two booking on and two booking off duty.

One day, at two o'clock, the signalman coming on duty was a relief man, Vince W. The two youths were taking advantage of a quiet spell by playing a game of skittle. They had only one skittle and one wooden ball. Vince came in and hung up his great coat and his food bag and greeted his mate. The two men talked train business for a minute or two while Vince signed his name in the train register and watched the two lads larking about. Said Jim, his own lad, 'Fancy a game Vince?'

Now Vince played skittles for a team in the nearby seaside town, and fancied his luck. As he hesitated the other boy Paul said, 'It's OK to play to knock down nine of them but it takes a good player to just hit the one!' This was too much for a dedicated Somerset skittler and Vince said, 'Right, give me that ball.' Jim rolled the ball to him and Vince took aim and knocked the skittle over. 'You couldn't do it again,' said Paul, 'it's just beginners luck.' 'Give me that ball,' said Vince, 'and we'll see.'

Jim rolled the ball to him and Vince took careful aim. He realised that the skittle was different because he could see it so easily. But no warning bell rang in his head and he let the ball fly. The bottle of milk that young Paul had just substituted for the skittle flew into fragments and milk covered the floor. Vince, astonished by the mess, walked up to the shattered bottle, saw what type it was, and walked up to his food bag and put his hand in. 'No milk! Paul,' he roared. 'Come here,' but Paul was already on the station platform and he wasn't stopping.

Bomb Scares

I booked on in Bristol at one o'clock, got my gear and walked to the platforms. I worked the 13:15 express to Paddington where we arrived at 15:35. (I was to work the 17:15 return to Bristol and Weston-super-Mare). I stacked away my rail letters and went to the guard's room which at the time was on the Mezzanine* floor above the "lawn"** and backing on to the Royal Hotel. As I went in, everyone else was coming out. I wondered why and asked. 'Bomb scare,' answered one. I went on in. I was going to make a can of tea whatever happened. I unpacked my can and tea container. From the doorway the man acting as warden called, 'Come on,' urgently; I said, 'You go on - I'll come as soon as I've made tea.' He repeated his request and I said, 'Bugger the IRA I am going to make tea.' I did so and leisurely walked down the stairs with my kit around my shoulders and a full can of freshly brewed tea in my left hand. Now I realised that I had not been told where to take shelter, so I headed for the subway leading to Praed Street underground station - put my kitbag on the floor; sat on it and proceeded to sugar and milk my can of tea.

Two cups of tea and two sandwiches later I looked around me, and I was appalled at my own stupidity. Facing me in the centre of the subway was an empty showcase, it was hexagonal with glass on each side. Behind me was another with enough glass if it shattered not only to kill me, but to render my corpse unrecognisable. I picked up everything and went further down the subway where there was no glass. When I had finished my tea and had a smoke I began to hear movements in the main station, and went up to find life was restarting. I made my way to platform eight and some minutes later a train ran in, which was to form the 17:15 back to Weston-super-Mare. I got my gear into the van and when the cleaners had done with the coaches, I prepared for the return journey. We had plenty of time to do everything, and at 17:15, to the second, I gave the right away and we drew out of Paddington.

Outside the great station canopy we swung across to the down main line. It was a nice warm evening and I stayed at my window looking at the well-known landmarks; watching the signals ahead. We came level with the new flats at Kensal Rise and there was an almighty explosion somewhere at the rear of them. Though I looked everywhere I could see nothing damaged, but a billow of dust was rising behind the flats through there was no sound of breaking glass. More of this I cannot tell you, for although I searched the newspapers, and asked numerous questions the next day in Paddington, nobody could tell me anything.

I have always felt a little uneasy when I think about the explosion.

*   A floor suspended between two others.

** Area at the end of the platforms at Paddington.

Permissive Block

In the days of semaphore signals, most of the tracks were worked on the absolute block system. This ensured that in each section of track could be only one train at a time. Colour light signalling has the same effect but works in a different way. The section roughly speaking was the gap between two signal-boxes, this is not completely accurate, but is a good guide. There was another system known as permissive block, which allowed trains (other than passenger trains) to travel nose to tail. There were many miles of such tracks in places like Pilning to Severn Tunnel and again from there to Newport. At other places it took the form of running loops at places like Trowbridge, Keynsham, Hele and Bradninch, Bulls Lock and Hay Lane.

The distinguishing mark for such tracks was a circle upon a semaphore signal. At every entrance to such tracks was the signal with a cricle or with a shorter arm and there was always some form of warning as to how many trains were already in the section, sometimes the signalman verbally warned the driver and sometimes a number appeared on an opal glass plate at the signal controlling the entrance to such a section. There were however human failures on such lines causing troubles. I saw one such accident one day.

A fast vacuum fitted freight train was running on the main line one morning on a piece of track where it would never normally need to be diverted. On the railway the word 'normally' has to be treated with great caution. On this day the signal for diversion to the permissive block line was off and the signalman was standing at his window waiting to tell the driver of the position of the previous train. The driver of the fast freight did not distinguish which signal he had off; he just knew he had one.

The swaying of the high wheeled locomotive as it passed over the junction joints was his first knowledge of something wrong, and he applied his brakes, but he had only one third vacuum fitted brakes and the heavy tail of the train pushed the front portion. Nothing was derailed on the crossover points with great luck, but then the vacuum hit the heavy slow freight in front, and there was chaos.

The guard of the slow freight had seen the whole thing happen and had jumped from his van. He saved his life, for his van was smashed to matchwood. The brand new Standard-type locomotive had its bogie broken off and considerable other damage but the driver and fireman escaped serious injury. Half a dozen wagons on the heavy freight were derailed and another half-dozen on the vacuum freight. The guard of the latter sustained head wounds and arm and shoulder bruising. There is no such thing as 'regularly' or 'normally' on the railway; one must be prepared for anything.

The Pregnant Lady

One Saturday in the summer of 1972, I waited on Plymouth station for the 'up Cornishman' which on Saturday only was booked to run non-stop from Plymouth to Chesterfield; at least as far as the public were concerned. Actually it had also to stop at Bristol to change crews, but this was not in the timetable. The train arrived, and I swapped information with the Penzance guard and relieved him, then we were on our way.

I strolled through the train as we climbed Hemerdon Bank to see all was in order. A lady opened the door of a first class compartment and called , 'Guard.' I turned and went in. She said, 'I have a seat reservation and it has this number on but it should be for second class.' I examined the reservation and found it was correctly numbered but wrongly classed as she had told me. I said, 'May I see your ticket,' and she produced a ticket - Plymouth to Paddington. Wrong train!

She asked where we were stopping, thinking she could get off and join her own train which was following. When I told her the situation she became very agitated and I began to take note of her. She was a very good looking woman in her forties and she was far advanced in pregnancy. (I found afterwards she was within 2 weeks of the expected birth). Her husband was waiting for her in London and would be very concerned if she didn't turn up.

I could of course take her off at Bristol when I was relieved; but the probability was that we would be relieved in the middle road where there was no platform. Not at all a suitable place to disembark the expectant mother, for the step-boards of a passenger train are nearly five feet off the ground. There are steps from the brake van, and handrails, but it is necessary to come down facing inwards to the van.

The lady told me she wanted some lunch, so I showed her the restaurant car and advised her to return to the first class seat when she had finished. I thought about how to get her to turn and get down from the brake van, for I would have the assistance of the Derby guard when he relieved me. When we had passed Uphill Junction I fetched her and her cases back to the rear van. We chatted a while and she seemed less agitated when I displayed a confidence I did not entirely feel. As we came up to Victoria Park I looked out for the signals to see what route we would be taking, and to my great relief I saw that we were going into a platform. I got the lady out onto the platform; showed her where the telephones were, and suggested that she ring her husband before catching the 15:15 train to London.

I had at least one satisfied customer that day.

Uses Of Chewing Gum

The Blue Pullmans had been in use many years when I joined the link*. The spares were running low, and since a date had already been decided for phasing them out, no new spares were ordered. Thus sets phased out from other areas were brought to Old Oak Common to be cannibalised. The Blue Pullmans had one advantage not enjoyed by any other type of train; they had a travelling technician. They were very good at their job but frequently we had to rely on sheer ingenuity from them to get home.

One evening working on the 17:15 from Paddington, my driver rang the telephone in the van and asked if the technician was there. I said no but I would get him and could I give him a message? He said, 'Yes, tell him No. 1 engine is racing and I can't shut it down.' I went to the restaurant car kitchen where I knew the technician was repairing some part of the cooking equipment. I gave him the driver's message, 'Oh yes,' he said, felt in his pocket, brought out a packet of chewing gum and put a stick in his mouth. 'This,' he said indicating at the packet, 'is what it needs!' I went with him to the van thinking he was leg pulling again.

'Come on!' he said and opened the engine room door. A blast of noise from the racing No. 1 engine hit us as we went into the inferno. The technician took the well chewed gum from his mouth and stuck it hard on the end of the control rod. The engine cut right out immediately, as he pressed the gum on the balance rod. Then, as he let go, the engine came up to normal running speed.

He had of course to order a new part as soon as we arrived, but ingenuity is what got us home.

* See Glossary

Bananas

In the days of steam the 'Bristolian' used to leave Temple Meads at 4:15 pm and run via Badminton non-stop to Paddington in an hour and forty-five minutes. It had to have a clear run in order to pass Wootten Basset Junction before the train which left at 4:00 pm travelling via Bath and Chippenham. In those days Avonmouth was the principal port for the banana trade of this country. For the London line specials, the route was via Filton West Junction, Stoke Gifford and Badminton and sometimes they could get involved with the schedule of the Bristolian.

Now, banana vans of the period were a bit odd in several respects; they were steam heated and vacuum braked, and though heavily insulated, weighed only slightly over seven tons each. With their load they seldom exceeded eleven tons and were usually less. They were permitted to travel at 60 miles per hour. With a decent engine and 50 or less vans, they could frequently reach this maximum speed. A banana special left Old Yard Avonmouth one summer afternoon bound for London with 50 vans and the ubiquitous 'Hall Class' engine. It pulled out of Gloucester Road at five minutes to four, the crew had their minds set on following the 'Bristolian' from Stoke Gifford. This would give them a clear run. But when they reached Filton West Junction, where the distant signal for Stoke Gifford West was situated, that signal was off. I should explain here for non railway people that a distant signal (painted yellow with a fish tail cut out and a black chevron) indicates that all the other signals belonging to that signal-box are also off.

The driver and the guard looked at their watches. It was five minutes past four; ten minutes in front of the 'Bristolian'. The driver opened the throttle and the guard sat tight in the van observing the signals. Coming up to Stoke Gifford West, the distant signal for the East box which was a lower arm on the West home was off, and the 'Hall' came up the hill and out on to the main line gathering speed.

Now it was a matter of where the 'banana' would be diverted, for it obviously could not get far in front of the 'Bristolian'. On the Badminton line there were plenty of places were the train could be side-tracked. By the time it passed East signal-box it had reached its maximum permitted speed and next came the little box at Winterbourne which closed down each afternoon at four. These signals were all clear and so were those for Coalpit Heath. It could be run on to up line at Westerleigh West Junction or into the siding at Wapley Common; but Westerleigh let it run and Wapley Common had switched out and gone home.

Now came the greatest surprise. Chipping Sodbury had long platform loops and it was as far as any of the crew of the 'banana special' expected to get in front of the express. But the distant signal was off and the special went through at high speed and dived headlong into the great tunnel. The driver and guard at opposite ends of the train checked their watches. It was four-fifteen. The 'Bristolian' would be leaving Temple Meads. They emerged from the tunnel and sped up the deep cutting.

The Badminton distant signal came into sight and it was off! They went through Badminton as if the devil was chasing them. It was four twenty-two. The 'Bristolian' was passing Winterbourne. They tore along at top speed and came in sight of the Hullavington distant signal. It was on. The driver eased the throttle and gently braked, for the entrance to the loop was speed restricted. As the van came opposite the telephone, the guard stepped off and rang the phone. He gave the signalman the 'train arrived complete' message. The signalman said 'thanks' and put the phone down somewhere but not on the hook, for the guard heard the block telegraph bells, two pause one (train out of section) one ring (call attention) answered - four bells (is line clear for 'Bristolian') -answered 'about twenty-seconds' then two bells (trains entering section). The guard rolled a cigarette and lit it, then walked the 50 yards to his van. As he pulled himself aboard, the 'Bristolian' flashed by very, very close! A few weeks later, the top-speed of the banana vans was reduced to forty-five miles an hour.

The driver of the special here described went with some others to see a demonstration film on safety and afterwards he told his guard that the film frightened him. He saw for himself that at forty-five miles an hour there was less than an inch of flange holding the wheel of the banana van on the track. 'I never dreamt,' said he, 'that we worked to such narrow margins; at the old speed of sixty miles an hour a coincidence of a sharp curve and one bad joint could have caused a derailment.'

Elsinore

I once went on holiday to Denmark, to the town of Elsinore (or Helsingor) where the great castle of which Shakespeare wrote is now a museum. What intrigued me was the tramline and the ferries. The trams (in pairs) started from just outside the main station and ran through the streets of the town and alongside the ship repair yards. Here they turned into miles of woodland and finally at Julebaek ran onto a very fine beach. The ferries gave a fantastic service across the Oresund to the Swedish port of Halsingborg.

During the day there was a ferry every 15 minutes. There were three docks, each in turn was loading a ferry, tying one up or dispatching one. There was no shouting, no whistles, no orders to be heard; unless there was fog and they didn't seem to get much of that.

A train from the south would arrive in the station which was a terminus. The station pilot engine would remove the last three coaches and pull them back over the quay points. A shunter would select the points required for one of the docks and the international coaches would emerge onto the quay and disappear aboard the appropriate ship in less than five minutes. Their square white destination boards showed 'Paris, Brussels, Stockholm' or similar. The shunters went aboard and clipped the locks on the coach wheels and took the pilot engine away inside another five minutes. It was all done without obvious orders, with no whistles or klaxon horns, and with the greatest quiet efficiency that I have ever seen. The loading of freight vehicles was just as efficiently done. It was speed without haste, about half a dozen wagons at a time, and the transfer effective and swift.

The Postmen's Strike

The postmen went on strike in 1971. It was their first strike since the revenge legislation following the General Strike of 1926 had forbidden civil servants to take such action. Their union had therefore no strike fund and though their wives drew social security money they all suffered considerable deprivation because of their stand. The disgusting Tory press screamed in their headlines that strikers should not get any state aid at all.

In the middle of the strike I was one day working the 10:30 Penzance to Leeds (the Cornishman) and I arrived at Taunton. A porter came along with two naval-style kitbags full to the tops and put them in my van. I was suspicious of these bags and examined them closely through the lace holes at their tops. I could see that they were stuffed with letters. I turned to the porter, 'Take these things out,' I said; for reply he shut the van doors. I was then forced to open the doors myself and haul the heavy kit bags out on to the platform. As I did so a typical 'Colonel Algernon Fitz-Maurice' arrived.(The only thing missing was a monocle) with a 'do as you are told - put those bags back in the van.'

He then started to threaten and bluster that he would immediately report my action direct to Paddington. I had been a little unsure of myself when throwing the bags out of the van, inspite of my sympathies with the postmen and in spite of my union's instruction that we were not to carry any form of mail; but the threats put my back up and I told the monocle-less wonder that I was in charge of this train. I could now see the lengths to which these types would go to frustrate the efforts of the postmen.

The inspector came up to see what all the kerfuffle was about and he gave his permission to leave and I gave the driver the "right away". As we pulled out, the "colonel", in fury, called out that he would put the bags on the next train anyway; and I told him I would see he didn't. To that end when we arrived in Bristol I went immediately to my union representative who made sure that this particular blackleg activity ceased.

I never heard anything from 'Colonel Algernon thingamy etcetera' .

Railway Workers

The Porters

The average non-railwayman's idea of the duties of a porter seems to end at the carrying of the passengers' luggage. With the exception of the London main termini, nothing could be further from the truth. Duties varied with each station, but among them were; washing out mess rooms, offices and waiting rooms; cleaning windows; bill sticking; whitening platform edges; laying and lighting fires and cleaning the grates; booking tickets prior to the arrival of the booking clerk and after his departure; brushing the platforms; booking up parcels; loading and unloading mails; acting as ground signalman in an emergency; cleaning and trimming tail lamps and filling up the oil barrels; cleaning and filling signal lamps; collecting tickets; oiling station barrows; fitting train roof labels and paper window labels; filling train lavatory tanks; sorting, collecting and disposing of train letters; assisting the local guard with shunting; closing wagon doors; sheeting and roping wagons; loading and unloading livestock; washing-out horse boxes and cattle trucks; tending the weighbridge; cleaning urinals and lavatories; relieving the next higher grades for sickness or holidays and answering enquiries. If they had any time left over they might carry passengers' luggage.

The Signalmen

The signalmen were, in general, the rules experts. They often had to prevent other staff from making errors, through their knowledge. Of course there were knowledgable drivers, guards, inspectors etc, but the signalmen were generally the best. Every signal-box had some special instructions which were listed above the bell shelf, due to the position, or to distances from neighbouring boxes or to special features of the area such as catch points, swing bridges, tunnels etc. or even in one place I know of, what to do when the sea washed over the track.

On the shelf were the bells, which were rung from the neighbouring boxes, and varied in number from two to six. Their tones were all different, and this was achieved by having bells of many varied shapes. Even so, I have seen a signalman check as to which bell had just rung, by putting his finger on the rim where a tiny vibration might be felt for a couple of seconds after the bell had rung. There was also a bell key (like a morse key) for every line to which he could dispatch a train and there was block instrument with two pegs and reminder flaps to each track.

If his box was at the beginning of a single line he had a staff or token instrument for each single line. These had a bell push in their construction and were a complete block instrument in themselves. There was a wide variety of other in-

Bristol West Signal-Box 1910. (The old manual signal-box). The white levers were spares in case the track lay-out was altered.

struments which might or might not be supplied. Many of these were track circuit instruments of many different types, but all having the function of showing the position of the train. The best of these was an illuminated diagram where lights were displayed on a map of the box control area. Manual frames varied to extremes for size. On a certain branch line there were two boxes of only six levers. But the junction box at one end was 135 levers and at the other end 80 levers.

The signalman had to observe every train passing him for loose loads, doors undone, or any other possible danger, and to check that the tail lamp had passed him, for this was the signal that the whole train had passed complete and that the section through which it had passed was in fact now clear. Other staff envied the signalmen the comfort of their boxes, but their responsibilities were very great.

On the lower grades of signal-boxes were some far out in the country and some in very exposed places. These men weren't too badly off once they had arrived, but sometimes their journeys to work were long, and these places were often quite primitive. There was often no running water supply; the box would be supplied with a couple of drinking water cans, which were exchanged daily by the guards of the local freight. There was often no water-closet, but a chemical one outside the box, not so nice on a snowy night! These country boxes received their instructions and daily notices - thrown from a passing passenger train. They were warned in advance by telephone to look out for these packets; if they were reasonably heavy everything would go fine, but it might happen that the envelope was thin and light and blew away and many were lost in this way. Some experienced guards would put a stone in the envelope to prevent its loss, but more than one window was broken in this way.

Once a week, laundry was exchanged by the freight guard; this was usually towels, dusters and sponge cloths. The men used a duster or sponge cloth on the steel levers, otherwise the sweat of their hands would rust the levers, whereas the dusters kept them polished.

It should be emphasised that these boxes were a small minority, and of course they are very rare indeed today, because of the spread of colour light signalling.

Driver on large steam locomotive.

Driver on more comfortable diesel unit.

The Drivers

The drivers throughout the years have had to show great adaptability because of the changes that have taken place. Before and during the Second World War, they dealt with many types of steam locomotives in their own company and during the conflict often drove engines which had 'strayed' from other lines. During this time the condition of the locomotives deteriorated as repairs piled up. The drivers and their firemen struggled on. Locomotives arrived with their firebars jammed together with clinker, which either had to be cleared and the fire restarted (imagine the delay) or struggle on unable to keep a sufficient head of steam.

After the war came the utility locos, standardised types, with no friends at all. The Western had converted some of their 28-class locos (2-8-0) to oil firing but as soon as was possible the idea was scrapped. Two gas turbine engines appeared; they were noisy brutes and could be heard and smelled in the coaches some way back. New standard steam engines the Sulzer diesels, the diesel rail cars, and the warship class diesels, arrived. Some drivers had to learn to drive them all, and so it has gone on ever since. Each of these locomotives also had a different maximum load, in fact different maximum loads for different types of train.

With the steam locomotives the drivers frequently roasted in front of the fire, and froze behind. The cabs had to be open at the back to allow the fireman to tend the fire. Many men suffered from varicose veins because of standing on steel plates constantly vibrating beneath them. Many men got hot ash in their eyes, when, the cab window having steamed or sooted up, they had to put their head out to make sure of a signal. The diesel locomotives of course were a great deal more comfortable; there wasn't much 'romance of steam' for the driver.

The amount of route knowledge required was very great. When the colour light signals began to spread, completely new layouts came into use and rendered a driver's route knowledge for that area obsolete overnight. He had to learn it all again and again. They needed a sense of humour at such times and most of them had it and survived.

The Shunters

Van|60 Wagons|Loco   Loco|60 Wagons|Van

The siding holds five wagons, or loco and two wagons. Shunt one train past the other! This is the old chestnut of a puzzle which used to be shown to every aspiring shunter. If he was going to be any good as a shunter he should solve the puzzle in no more than five minutes, because as a shunter he would spend his whole time solving puzzles. If he were an average shunter, he would spend years changing turns at 10:00 pm, 6:00 am and 2:00 pm. He would spend time shunting wagons into correct order for a certain train, only to be told by the guard, 'Sorry mate we've got a full load now, can't pick up.' Since few trains had the same stops even if they were travelling in the same direction, the wagons shunted out laboriously for one train had to be rearranged for another.

Then the shunter had to arrange the correct balance of vacuum braked vehicles for fast freight trains. These trains were formed up double ended thus: locomotive - vacuum fitted A depot, vacuum fitted B depot, vacuum fitted C depot, non vacuum C depot, non vacuum B depot, non vacuum A depot, brake van. Therefore if the shunter was not prepared with the correct proportion of vacuum braked vehicles, the train might have to be shunted into three portions with loss of time. Since some fast freight trains were only allowed about ten minutes in which to detach and attach traffic, the shunter had to do his best with the least number of movements possible.

His knowledge of British geography had to be vast, and he had to select trains to take the really long distance traffic as far as possible with the least number of transfers. He had to know what types of traffic were forbidden on certain trains, and which traffic could not be mixed i.e. explosives, dangerous chemicals, livestock, inflamables such as petrol, and atomic flasks. He had to accept last minute instructions from the control, who always seemed to wait until everything had been shunted out before sending contrary instructions and he had to do it at night with sparse yard lighting, and an oil burning hand lamp. Then there was the British weather: the rain, hail, sleet, snow, fog, frost and sometimes even sunshine. Nothing could be allowed to stop the work, though fog or falling snow could slow it up, and make everything late.

Most men had two sets of waterproof coats and leggings and frequently needed both sets on a really wet turn. When wet, these macs were very heavy, and after eight hours work in the rain, actually caused fatigue by their sheer weight; add to all this the dirt and the grease of heavy screw couplings and the dangers of working between wagons: - it seems a wonder that anyone took the job.

The Guards

The guards were the travelling shunters and the travelling clerks. They kept a record of the loading and the timekeeping of the train, and this was known as the journal.

They were responsible for loading the train correctly and for informing the driver correctly. They ordered bank engines where the load necessitated it, or if requested by the driver.

The calculation of load for a passenger train was simple - just add together the weights of the vehicles. However, the passenger guard had to contend with varying gradients and different classes of locomotives.

The freight guard's calculations were more complicated. His train could be carrying three classes of traffic, plus empties, and all had proportionate weights. Additionally there were several dozen types of special vehicles, all of which had different load weights. These details had all to be entered on the journal, and corrected for each time traffic was attached and or detached.

The guards were supplied with pocket watches and kept the official times of the train. It is not generally understood that the driver was not supplied with a watch, but of course they all carried their own. It was a legitimate grievance of their's for many years. The guard had to understand the signals as did the driver. The freight guard needed an intimate knowledge of the gradients.

Toward the end of my career, the passenger guard had to collect, check, and issue tickets as required on trains. They were then called conductor guards. All had to know how to protect their train in an emergency, and this was quite complicated.

They were responsible for all safety measures on their trains. They had to see that all doors were properly fastened, materials roped down where necessary, all brakes released, and nothing projecting from their train. Like all other railwaymen they did it in all winds and weathers, and at every hour of the clock.

GWR guard in uniform. On his collar is written 'Guard' which was removed before the Second War. Probably 1920s. Note clerestory roofed coaches and wooden edged platforms.

Railway Terms and Slang

Bank ....A steep incline.

Banker ....An assistant locomotive used on these inclines.

Bay ....A dead-end line for passenger train working.

Blow up inside ....Make sure you are clear of the points and give three blasts on the whistle.

Blower ....The telephone.

Bobby or policeman ....Signalman

Bogie ....The four small leading wheels of a steam locomotive or the four wheels of either end of passenger rolling stock.

Booking boy ....A youth employed on very busy signal-boxes to record the passage of trains.

Box ....A signal cabin (manual).

Brew up or mash ....Make tea.

Butterfly ....The indicator at the end of a coach showing where the communication chain has been pulled.

Cabin ....Mess and locker room.

Catch points ....Spring loaded points inserted in steep gradients. Trains may pass in the right direction by pressure on the springs but will be derailed if running backwards.

Compo or composite ....A coach with first and second class seats.

Detonator placer machine ..A signal-box lever painted black and white enabling the signalman to put detonators on the track in an emergency.

Distant signal ....A yellow painted signal with a fish tail cut out and a black chevron. The light is yellow-on; green-off.

Dock ....A dead-end road with a platform for parcel loading.

Double home ....A system where men worked outwards one day and back the next (now abandoned).

Down line ....The track from London.

Dummy or doll ....Ground signal.

Facing points (manual) .....Points where the engine arrives at the tongue end first. These are kept to a minimum on main lines and then are equipped with locks and fouling bars.

Facing point locks ....These are operated from the signal-box and consist of a heavy steel bar and a choice of two slots in which it fits, according to the setting of the points.

Fouling bars ....These are usually about 45 feet long and prevent the facing point being moved while the vehicle is standing upon them.

The Gang ....Permanent way Engineers.

Gantry ....A convenient method of providing signals on a large number of tracks by building a bridge over all lines.

Ground frame ....In effect a miniature signal frame. Methods of working varied. Sometimes one or more keys could be released by arrangement with the signalman (by telephone). These were necessary where the points concerned were beyond the agreed distance for manual operation. Sometimes the key was kept in the box and had to be taken from, and returned there. On single lines the key for operation was in the end of the single line staff or token.

Hanging the pot on ....Deliberately delaying

Hot box ....A very dangerous condition where the axle-box bearings got very hot and start to melt. In the days of grease axle-boxes this was quite common. With plain bearing oil boxes it was less so; with modern roller bearing grease pressure packed boxes, it is virtually unknown.

Lights ....Signal (colour lights).

Links ....A number of duties where men work on a rota basis

Mileage (1) ....A system of payments to train crews as bonus for long distance working.

Mileage (2) ....The principal siding in a goods depot devoted to public use.

Number one ....First notice of disciplinary action.

Panel ....A modern electronic signal cabin.

Permanent way engineers ..The men who maintain the track.

Pilot working ....A method of working a single line where a token is not available. A member of staff acts as a human token.

Platform loop ....See running loop below, but with passenger platform.

Pony truck ....Two wheeled bogie (see bogie).

Raft (of wagons) ....A number of wagons which become assembled during shunting.

Refuge ....A siding into which a train has to be backed. This would be kept only for diverting trains and not used for other purposes.

Running loop ....Side track where a train may run in at one end and out at the other.

Sand drag ....A catch point leading to a long rail buried in sand thus usually avoiding derailment, though the vehicle is stopped by the sand.

Setter ....Guard's vacuum or air brake.

Shots ....Detonators.

Snatch ....A snatch occured with loose coupled trains as a result of the engine slipping then regaining traction.

Stop signal ....Any signal with a red arm and white band and a red light, including ground signals; a distant signal is not a stop signal.

Stick or Board ....Signal (semaphore).

Smokey Joes ....A staff café of a less salubrious nature.

Token or staff ....A metal key, colour coded, and named with the signal-boxes at each end of the section without which a driver may not enter a single line. Does not apply to colour light areas such as Severn Beach.

Track circuit block (TCB) . Track circuit block. The modern method of controlling the passage of trains by colour light signalling.

Track circuit
(older circuits) ....polarities (low voltage) when a train uses the track the circuit is completed via the wheels and axles. Indicators, wired in series, become operative. The two tracks are electrified at opposite

Tunnel ....An overhead enclosure of minimum length 2 chains (44 yards).

Unit ....Diesel multiple unit (usually three vehicles).

Up line ....The track towards London

The vans ....Break-down trains.